Ingrid Preedy

Besser in

Englisch

5. Klasse

Gymnasium

Cornelsen
SCRIPTOR

Über die Autorin:
Ingrid Preedy ist Britin. Sie hat langjährige Erfahrung als Englischlehrerin und ist auch in der Lehrerfortbildung tätig. Sie ist Autorin mehrerer Schulbücher und Unterrichtsmaterialien.

Bibliografische Information der Deutschen Nationalbibliothek
Die Deutsche Nationalbibliothek verzeichnet diese Publikation in der Deutschen Nationalbibliografie; detaillierte bibliografische Daten sind im Internet über http://dnb.d-nb.de abrufbar.

2. Auflage

Bibliographisches Institut GmbH
Dudenstraße 6, 68167 Mannheim

Redaktionelle Leitung: Constanze Schöder
Redaktion: lüra - Klemt & Mues GbR
Illustrationen: Dorina Teßmann
Herstellung: Annette Scheerer
Layoutkonzept: Horst Bachmann, Weinheim
Umschlaggestaltung: glas AG, Seeheim-Jugenheim
Satz/Layout: Ines Schiffel, Berlin
Druck und Bindung: orthdruk, Białystok
Printed in Poland

ISBN 978-3-411-87024-0

Liebe Schülerin, lieber Schüler,

du hast hier ein Buch zum **Lernen, Wiederholen und Üben** in der Hand.

- ▷ Die Themen sind in kleinen, verständlichen Schritten aufbereitet.
- ▷ Schaffe dir parallel zu diesem Buch ein Arbeitsheft an, in das du hineinschreiben kannst.
- ▷ Ein Lösungsheft hilft dir, deine Ergebnisse zu kontrollieren.
- ▷ Mit der beiliegenden CD und vielen Übungen dazu kannst du dein Hörverstehen trainieren. Folgender Hinweis zeigt dir, wo du die CD verwenden musst:

Track

Mit diesem Buch kannst du auf zweierlei Weise arbeiten:

1. Möglichkeit:

Wenn du dich im Fach Englisch insgesamt ein wenig unsicher fühlst, solltest du das Buch von vorn bis hinten durcharbeiten. Nimm dir aber nicht zu viel auf einmal vor. Bearbeite lieber kleinere Abschnitte und arbeite dafür regelmäßig, vielleicht sogar täglich.

2. Möglichkeit:

Vielleicht kommst du eigentlich gut zurecht, hast aber einige Lücken? Kläre genau, am besten mithilfe deiner Lehrerin oder deines Lehrers, wo deine Lücken sind. Sieh im Inhaltsverzeichnis nach, wähle einzelne Abschnitte aus und arbeite sie durch.

GOOD TO KNOW | **Zum Arbeiten mit diesem Buch**

- ▶ Manche Aufgaben kannst du im Buch lösen. Benutze ein **Arbeitsheft**, wenn du viel schreiben musst.
- ▶ Bist du beim Lösen der Übungsaufgaben unsicher, schau dir die **Beispiele** dazu noch einmal an.
- ▶ Vergleiche deine Ergebnisse immer sorgsam mit denen im **Lösungsheft**. Überprüfe genau, was du falsch gemacht hast. Aus Fehlern kann man gut lernen.
- ▶ Bearbeite dieselben Aufgaben nach einigen Tagen noch einmal. Die **Wiederholung** schafft Sicherheit.

1 Sprache verstehen

Das musst du am Ende der Klasse 5 können:

- ▷ Einfache Fragen stellen
- ▷ Fragen beantworten
- ▷ Einfache Wendungen und Sätze grammatisch richtig schreiben
- ▷ Beschreiben, wo du wohnst
- ▷ Deine Schule und deine Freunde beschreiben

1.1 Wortart: Verb – Die Zeiten *(tenses)*

REMEMBER Das *simple present*

Du benutzt das *simple present*, um zu sagen, dass etwas immer gleich ist oder normalerweise passiert, z. B. jeden Tag, manchmal, öfter.

Signalwörter für das *simple present* sind z. B.: always, never, often, sometimes, usually, every day, every week, at the weekend, on Saturdays.

Das simple present lässt sich wirklich „einfach" bilden: Es entspricht dem Infinitiv – der Grundform des Verbs – außer bei *he, she, it*. Hier musst du ein s an den Infinitiv anfügen: Bei *he, she, it,* ein s muss mit.
Beispiele: to learn (= Infinitiv) – I learn, you learn, we learn, they learn
Aber: he learns

Leider kannst du nicht immer einfach ein s anhängen.
Ist der letzte Buchstabe des Wortes ein y, wird daraus -ies. Das gilt nicht, wenn ein Vokal *(a, e, i, o, u)* davorsteht.
Beispiele: I fly, he fl**ies**

Bei y nach einem Vokal wird ein einfaches s angehängt.
Beispiele: I play, aber: he play**s**; I buy, aber: he buy**s**

Bei allen Zischlauten *(ch, sh, tch)* muss -es angehängt werden.
Beispiel: I watch, he watch**es**

Aufpassen: I go → he go**es** I do → he do**es**

1 **Make sentences.**
Write the verb *play* in the right form.
Schreibe Sätze. Verwende die richtige Form des Verbs *play*.

EXAMPLE

The boys play cards after school.

1. Peggy plays in a football team.
2. Jack plays tennis on Saturdays.
3. The teacher plays Bingo with the pupils.
4. I play the piano.
5. Jack and Jill play cards every Friday.
6. My father plays tennis with my mother.

2 **Make sentences.**
Write the verb in the right form.
Schreibe Sätze. Verwende die richtige Form des Verbs.

David and Stephan (play) football. They (go) to training every Wednesday. They (play) with their friend, Calvin, after school. He (live) near the school. The boys (like) Calvin's mother. She always (have) milk and biscuits for them. Calvin (have) a lot of new computer games. His father (work) in a computer shop and often (bring) new games home for Calvin.

3 Say it in English.

Schreibe in dein Heft. Sage auf Englisch, dass ...

1. du den BVB magst.
2. deine Mutter Basketball spielt.
3. dein Freund ein Schwimmbad im Garten hat.
4. du manchmal samstags ins Kino gehst.
5. Herr Brown mit seiner Frau in einem Buchladen arbeitet.
6. sie immer am Wochenende im Garten arbeiten.

REMEMBER *Simple present*: Verneinung

Die Verneinung im *simple present* bildest du mit don't bzw. bei *he, she, it* mit doesn't.

Ausnahmen: is → isn't, are → aren't, can → can't, have → haven't, has → hasn't
Beispiel: They **don't** play hockey. He **doesn't** play hockey.
Aber: You **can't** play hockey today. She **can't** play hockey today.

4 Make sentences. Use *don't* or *doesn't* in the right form.

Schreibe Sätze. Verwende die richtige Form von *don't* oder *doesn't*.

EXAMPLE

Tim and Robert	*don't*	*play tennis on Saturdays.*
Janet	*doesn't*	*learn German.*

1. The girls don't like football.
2. My teacher doesn't live in my street.

3. The teachers ______ play enough games in lessons.

4. My friend ______ like spinach.

5. We ______ learn Chinese at school.

6. Fish ______ fly, they swim.

7. Peter ______ come from Germany.

5 Complete the sentences.

Ergänze die Sätze mithilfe der Bilder. Schreibe die Verneinung auf.

1. I like dogs but I ______ .

2. My father plays golf but he ______ .

3. Tigers live in India but they ______ .

4. My mother can ride a bike but she ______ .

5. I have got a rabbit but I ______ .

6. He has got a bike but he a boat.

6 Say it in English.

Schreibe in dein Heft. Sage auf Englisch, dass …

1. du Wellensittiche (= budgies) nicht magst.
2. dein Hund nicht in einem Korb schläft.
3. deine Freunde keine Haustiere haben.
4. deine Schildkröte Hunde nicht mag.
5. dein Vater die Tiere nicht füttert.

REMEMBER *Simple present*: Fragen

Fragen bildest du mit do bzw. bei *he, she, it* mit does.

Beispiel: **Do** you learn English at your school?
Does he learn English at his school?

Ausnahmen: is, can, have, has
Can you speak English? Are you English?

7 Ask questions.

Schreibe die Fragen in dein Heft. Benutze KEINE Fragewörter.

EXAMPLE

His dog is eleven years old. *Is his dog eleven years old?*
Peter's guinea pig can swim. *Can …*

1. The big black dog lives next to the school. *Does …*
2. The zoo is next to the library.
3. An elephant can eat 100 apples every day.
4. The pet shop sells rabbits.
5. Susan's cat eats oranges.
6. Lots of zoo animals are dangerous.
7. Elephants live in Africa.
8. Gordon likes to go to the zoo.

8 Ask in English.

Schreibe in dein Heft. Frage auf Englisch, ob …

1. du einen Hund haben kannst.
2. eine Schildkröte in einem Käfig lebt.
3. Goldfische nachts schwimmen.
4. Hamster schnell laufen können.

REMEMBER Häufigkeitsadverbien

Da du mit dem *simple present* sagen möchtest, dass etwas wiederholt passiert, gebrauchst du oft Häufigkeitsadverbien. Dazu gehören z. B.: often, always, sometimes, usually, never.

Diese Adverben stehen
→ nach dem Hilfsverb: I always go home after school.
→ direkt vor dem Vollverb: I can always ...
→ nach am, is, are: I am always going ...

Beispiel: Linda **always eats** cornflakes for breakfast.
Linda **has sometimes** got an apple in her school bag.
Linda **is always** hungry.

9 Mark the place to put the adverb of frequency.

Markiere die Stelle mit einem Haken, an die das Häufigkeitsadverb gehört.

EXAMPLE

(often) *Gordon ✓ goes ☐ to the zoo ☐ at the weekend.*

1. (sometimes) He ☐ looks at ☐ all the animals.
2. (never) He ☐ brings ☐ food ☐ for the animals.
3. (always) He ☐ buys ☐ food from the zoo ☐ for the animals.
4. (sometimes) He ☐ takes ☐ photos of the baby animals.
5. (never) He ☐ bangs ☐ on the cages.
6. (sometimes) He ☐ takes ☐ a picnic ☐ with him.
7. (always) He ☐ goes ☐ home half an hour ☐ before the zoo closes.

10 Choose the right answer.

Welche Antwort ist richtig? Setze einen Haken (✓) in das richtige Kästchen.

1. When do you write to your grandmother?
   - ☐ I write to my grandmother every week.
   - ☐ I write to my grandmother at home.
   - ☐ I write to my grandmother because it is her birthday.

2. Where is Tom?
   - ☐ He is my friend.
   - ☐ He is at my father's house.
   - ☐ He is thirteen.

3. Can I see your homework, please?
   - ☐ Yes, it is my homework.
   - ☐ No, it is my homework.
   - ☐ I'm sorry, but it is at home.

4. Why is Janet so angry?
   - ☐ Yes, she is.
   - ☐ Because her brother has got her MP3 player.
   - ☐ No, but she is my friend.

5. How long does it take to get to school?
   - ☐ About fifteen minutes by bike.
   - ☐ I go by bus.
   - ☐ It starts at 8 o'clock and finishes at 2 o'clock.

6. What time do you get up in the morning?
   - ☐ At seventeen.
   - ☐ At seven o'clock. ☐ At midnight.

7. Is there a post office in your town?
   - ☐ It is over there.
   - ☐ There are two.
   - ☐ Yes, it is.

8. What is your school like?
   - ☐ Yes, I like it.
   - ☐ It is old and small.
   - ☐ Yes, it is.

11 Fill in the gaps. Choose the right verb. Write the verb in the right form.
Fülle die Lücken aus. Wähle das passende Verb. Schreibe die richtige Form des Verbs auf.

drink *eat* *go* *have* *watch*

get up *go* *take* *leave*

meet *play* *take* *want* *listen*

Anne always (1) gets up at 8 o'clock on Saturdays. She (2) goes into the kitchen for breakfast. Her parents are there. She often (3) plays hockey at the weekend. Her father usually (4) goes with her and (5) watches the game. Anne and her father always (6) listen to the weather report on the radio because they (7) have to know about the weather. They (8) leave the house at 9.15. Her father usually (9) eats sandwiches and coffee with him. Anne never (10) eats before a hockey game but she always (11) drinks a lot of water. She sometimes (12) takes the bus to the hockey game so she can (13) meet her friends. They always (14) have good fun on the bus.

12 Say it in English.

Schreibe in dein Heft. Sage auf Englisch, dass ...

1. dein Hund öfters im Garten herumrennt.
2. dein Wellensittich niemals im Wohnzimmer fliegt.
3. du manchmal mit dem Nachbarshund zum Park gehst.
4. du deinem Goldfisch immer frisches Wasser gibst.
5. dein Hund immer in deinem Zimmer schläft.

REMEMBER Das *present progressive*

Du benutzt das *present progressive*, um zu sagen, dass etwas gerade in diesem Moment passiert.

Merke: Signalwörter sind z. B.: now, at the moment, Look!, Listen!

Du bildest das *present progressive* mit *am, is, are* + verb + -ing

Beispiel: I am learning English at the moment.
You are learning English now.
He/She is learning English at the moment.
We are learning English at the moment.
Look! Jack is coming.

GOOD TO KNOW Besonderheiten

Leider kannst du nicht immer einfach -ing anhängen.
Wenn der letzte Buchstabe des Wortes ein e ist, fällt das e weg.
Beispiel: I give → I am giving
Wenn die letzten drei Buchstaben Konsonant + Vokal + Konsonant sind, wird der letzte Buchstabe verdoppelt.
Beispiel: I stop → I am stopping
ie am Ende wird zu y.
Beispiel: I lie → I am lying

1 Write down the present progressive forms of these verbs.
Schreibe die *present progressive*-Formen dieser Verben auf.

ask → ____ bring → ____

come → ____ do → ____

draw → ____ get → ____

hope → ____ look → ____

miss → ____ run → ____

try → ____ wave → ____

2 Put the verb in brackets in the right tense: simple present or present progressive.
Setze das Verb in die richtige Form: *simple present* oder *present progressive*. Schreibe in dein Heft.

1. The lesson (begin) at 8 o'clock every morning.
2. I never (go) out on Friday evenings.
3. He (come) to visit my mother every day.
4. She (look) for a new bike.
5. He (learn) French at the moment.
6. Colin's marks are not very good at the moment. He (not work) hard enough.
7. At the moment Lucy (work) on her project.
8. It (rain) very often in the south of England.
9. Look! The children (drink) beer.
10. The shop (open) at 8 o'clock every Sunday.
11. How often (your Dad cook) dinner?
12. They usually (have) dinner at 7 o'clock.
13. I (not listen) to the radio very often.
14. He sometimes (go) to the park with his dog.
15. He usually (watch) TV on Sundays.
16. Can you hear that? Somebody (sing).

3 Write sentences about people and what they are doing at the moment.

Schreibe auf, was die verschiedenen Personen gerade machen.

4 Say it in English.

Schreibe in dein Heft. Sage es auf Englisch.

1. Du schaust im Moment Fußball im Fernsehen.
2. Arsenal spielt gegen Liverpool.
3. Im Moment gewinnt Arsenal.
4. Hört! Die Arsenal-Anhänger klatschen.
5. Schau! Owen läuft mit dem Ball zum Tor.

REMEMBER *Present progressive:* Verneinung

Die Verneinung bildest du mit not. Not steht nach der Form von be.
Beispiel: I am learning English / I am **not** learning German.

5 Negate these sentences.

Setze die Aussagesätze in die verneinte Form. Du kannst dabei die Langform von *be* benutzen. Schreibe die Sätze in dein Heft.

EXAMPLE

Tom is playing in his room. *He is not playing in his room.*

1. He is listening to his CDs.
2. He is doing his homework.
3. His friends are waiting for him.
4. Tom and his friends are playing football in the garden now.

REMEMBER *Present progressive:* Fragen

Fragen bildest du, indem du am, is, are an den Satzanfang stellst.
Beispiel: He **is** learning English. / **Is** he learning English?

6 Write the questions for these answers.
Schreibe die Fragen zu den Antworten.

1. Are you learning to ride a bike ? ✓
No, I am not learning to ride a bike. I am learning to skate.

2. Are yo going to ~~the~~ shopping ? ~~cat~~ ✗
Yes, I am. I always go shopping on Fridays.

3. Are You Painting the house ~~Do you like~~ drawing with collour? ✗
Yes, I am. Nice colour, isn't it? It is easy to paint a house.

4. Are you playing football today ? ✓
No, not today. Today is Saturday and I only play football on Sundays.

GOOD TO KNOW | **Welche Gegenwartsform?**

Das *present progressive* (die Verlaufsform) und das *simple present* (die einfache Gegenwart) im Vergleich

Das *present progressive* (die Verlaufsform der Gegenwart) benutzt du, um auszudrücken, dass jemand gerade in diesem Moment etwas tut. Die Handlung ist also noch nicht zu Ende.
Die *simple present* (die einfache Form der Gegenwart) benutzt du, wenn du ausdrücken möchtest, dass jemand etwas wiederholt (oft, regelmäßig, gelegentlich, jeden Tag/Monat/Sommer/Weihnachten) oder nie tut.

Signalwörter für das *present progressive* (die Verlaufsform) sind z. B.: at the moment, now, Look!, Listen!
Signalwörter für das *simple present* (die einfache Gegenwart) sind z. B.: always, often, sometimes, never, usually, every day, every week, every month.
Achtung: Es gibt einige Verben, die Zustände beschreiben und keine Aktivität ausdrücken, die normalerweise nur im *simple present* benutzt werden. Dazu gehören z. B.: be, believe, hate, hear, know, like, love, need, see, understand, want.

7 Which of these are the signal words for the present progressive?

Was sind typische Signalwörter für das *present progressive*? Mache einen Haken (✓) in die richtigen Kästchen.

1. Listen!
2. at the moment
3. every day
4. now
5. often
6. sometimes

8 Which of these are the signal words for the simple present?

Was sind typische Signalwörter für das *simple present*? Mache einen Haken (✓) in die richtigen Kästchen.

1. at the moment
2. every day
3. now
4. often
5. sometimes
6. just

9 Which sentences/questions use the simple present?

Welche Sätze/Fragen stehen im *simple present*? Mache einen Haken (✓) in die richtigen Kästchen.

1. Do you like maths?
2. We don't go to school by bike.
3. He is German.
4. She is learning German.
5. She is sitting on a chair.
6. Mary doesn't like swimming.
7. Is she talking on the phone again?
8. I can't play hockey.

10 Which sentences/questions use the present progressive?

Welche Sätze/Fragen stehen im *present progressive*? Mache einen Haken (✓) in die richtigen Kästchen.

1. She is doing her homework.
2. My father never makes breakfast.
3. I often take photos at school.
4. Is the boy playing in the garden?
5. Mr and Mrs Smith are not washing their car.
6. We have got a new car.
7. That is why we are washing it now.

11 Negate the following sentences.

Verneine die vorgegebenen Sätze. Schreibe in dein Heft.

EXAMPLE

He is playing computer games. *He is not playing computer games.*

1. He is looking at a photo.
2. I am repairing my bike.
3. Robert and Tim live in Frankfurt.
4. Peter collects picture postcards.
5. Our English teacher looks at our homework every day.

12 Put the verb in the right form of the present tense.

Setze das Verb in die richtige Gegenwartsform. Beachte dabei vorhandene Signalwörter.

1. (go) Tim usually ______ to school by bus. But look! Today he ______ by bike.
2. (play) Jack never ______ in the street. He always ______ in the park.

3. (bring) Look! The postman ________ the post now. He usually ________ the post at 11 o'clock.
4. (run) Man: Hey! Your big, black dog ________ after that bus.
Woman: Yes, I know. It always ________ after buses. It never ________ after cars, only buses.
5. (buy) Mrs Black always ________ her bread from the shop at the corner. She never ________ her bread from the supermarket.
6. (repair) It is the weekend and Mr Jackson ________ his car.
He always ________ his car on Saturdays. It is a very old car!
7. (wash) All the people in our street ________ their cars on Saturdays.
Nobody ________ their car on a Sunday.
8. (work) My neighbour ________ in the garden every week but at the moment he ________ in the house.
9. (leave) The bus usually ________ at 8 o'clock. But today it is late. It ________ now and the time is 8.20 a.m.
10. (get up) In Germany a lot of people ________ at 6 o'clock.
11. (go) Pat often ________ to school by car.
12. (watch) I ________ a nice film now.
13. (sing) Listen! Anne and Susan ________ a song.
14. (go) Angela sometimes ________ to a museum.
15. (play) We ________ a computer game at the moment.

13 Make questions in the present progressive with the verbs in brackets.
Schreibe Fragen im *present progressive*. Benutze die Verben in Klammern.

1. ______ Barbara ______ my book? (to read)
2. ______ Mandy ______ a book out of her bag? (to take)
3. ______ your friends ______ home from school? (to come)
4. ______ Ashley ______ on the computer? (to work)
5. ______ you ______ to music? (to listen)
6. ______ Nadine ______ at a picture? (to look)
7. ______ Eric and Bob ______ their friends? (to phone)
8. ______ the girl ______ the windows? (to open)

14 Choose the correct form. Tick (✓) the box.
Wähle die richtige Form. Setze einen Haken (✓) in das richtige Kästchen.

1. John plays ☐ is playing ☐ play ☐ are playing ☐ football at the moment.
2. Look! Mandy and Susan watch ☐ are watching ☐ is watching ☐ watches ☐ a film.
3. Every morning my mother is getting ☐ get ☐ gets ☐ are getting ☐ up at 6 o'clock.
4. Our class often write ☐ writes ☐ are writing ☐ is writing ☐ tests.
5. First I get up, then I have ☐ has ☐ is having ☐ am having ☐ breakfast.
6. The sun shines ☐ shine ☐ is shining ☐ are shining ☐ now.

15 Put the verb in brackets into the present progressive.
Setze das Verb in Klammern ins *present progressive*.

EXAMPLE

I am standing (stand) *in the rain.*

1. I ______ (work) hard for my test!
2. Colin ______ (go) to Berlin.
3. They ______ (have) a Chinese lesson at the moment.
4. We ______ (play) basketball right now.
5. She ______ (move) to Canada.
6. At the moment, we ______ (try) to learn our maths.
7. Linda ______ (think) about the film on TV.
8. I ______ (do) this exercise because it is good.
9. Why are you ______ (look) at me?
10. She ______ (listen) to that song.
11. They ______ (travel) to Paris by car.
12. He ______ (talk) about her.

16 Now write each sentence in the negative.
Schreibe jetzt alle Sätze von Aufgabe 15 in die negative Form um.
Schreibe in dein Heft.

EXAMPLE

I am standing (stand) *in the rain. I'm not standing in the rain.*

REMEMBER Das *going to-future*

Das *going to-future* wird verwendet, um über feste Absichten für die Zukunft zu sprechen oder über Dinge, von denen man absehen kann, dass sie passieren werden.

Das *going to-future* wird gebildet mit *am, is, are* + *going to* + verb

Beispiele: I am going to learn French at school next year.
He is going to play football this afternoon.
We are going to have spaghetti for dinner.
They are going to arrive at 4 o'clock.
Watch out! The ladder's going to break!
Look at those clouds! It's going to rain.
Help! I'm going to be sick.
You're going to get a bad mark if you don't work harder.

1 Complete the sentences and say what is going to happen next.

Ergänze die Sätze. Schreibe auf, was passieren wird.

sink *fall off* *break* *stop*

1. The man on the bike ______ .
2. Watch out! You ______ that plate.
3. That boat ______ if they're not careful.
4. Look! The policeman ______ that car.

2 Say it in English.

Schreibe in dein Heft. Sage auf Englisch, dass ...

1. du eine neue Federmappe kaufen willst.
2. dein Freund mit dir in die Stadt gehen wird.
3. ihr den Bus um 11.30 nehmen werdet.
4. deine Eltern euch um 12.00 in der Stadt treffen werden.

REMEMBER *going to-future:* **Verneinung**

Die Verneinung im *going to-future* wird mit not gebildet. Not steht nach der Form von be, genau wie beim *present progressive.*

Beispiel: I'm not going to learn French next year. I'm going to learn Chinese.

3 Write what the children are not going to do.

Schreibe in dein Heft, was die Kinder nicht vorhaben.

EXAMPLE

Carol ________ (not forget to feed) the rabbit.

Carol is not going to forget to feed the rabbit.

1. The boys ________ (not clean) their football boots in the kitchen.
2. Dan ________ (not put) the sand from the budgie's cage in the toilet.
3. The twins ________ (not forget) to do their homework.
4. Jack and Jill ________ (not eat) chocolate before dinner.
5. Tom ________ (not take) the bus to school. The school is only 10 minutes away.
5. The Thomson brothers ________ (not laugh) at the girls again.
6. The girls ________ (not write) letters in class.

4 Say it in English.

Schreibe in dein Heft. Sage auf Englisch, dass ...

1. du auf der Party nicht tanzen wirst. *I ...*
2. deine Freunde nicht auf die Party gehen werden. *My ...*
3. du nicht vergessen wirst, ein Geschenk mitzunehmen. *I ...*
4. du keine albernen Spiele spielen wirst. *I ...*
5. du nicht vor 20 Uhr zu Hause sein wirst. *I ...*

REMEMBER *going to-future:* **Fragen**

Fragen bildet man beim *going to-future,* indem man am, is, are an den Satzanfang stellt, genau wie beim *present progressive.*

Beispiel: He is going to learn French. / Is he going to learn French?

5 Ask in English.

Schreibe in dein Heft. Frage auf Englisch, ...

1. ob die Geschäfte heute um 7 Uhr schließen werden.
2. ob das neue Geschäft aufmachen wird.
3. ob ihr mir zum Geburtstag ein Kaninchen schenkt.
4. ob dir jemand beim Tragen des neuen Käfigs helfen wird.

6 Write down what the weather is going to be today.

Schreibe in dein Heft. Sage, wie das Wetter heute wird.

Berlin	Madrid	London	Paris	Oslo	Munich

30° C	20° C	5° C	35° C	5° C	25° C

EXAMPLE

Today it is going to be hot and sunny in Berlin.

1.2 Fragen

REMEMBER **Fragen bilden**

Fragen bildest du, indem du am, is, are an den Satzanfang stellst.
Beispiel: He **is** learning English. → **Is** he learning English?

Es gibt zwei Arten von Fragen:

- Entscheidungsfragen
- Fragen mit Fragewörtern bzw. Fragen nach dem Subjekt

1. Entscheidungsfragen

Bei Entscheidungsfragen (bei Fragen, bei denen die Antwort yes oder no erwartet wird) sind Subjekt und Verb einfach vertauscht.

Beispiele:

Is he English?	Can he swim?	Have you got a dog?
Yes, he is English.	No, he can't swim.	Yes, I have got a dog.

2. Fragen nach dem Subjekt

In Sätzen, in denen nach dem Subjekt des Satzes gefragt wird, benutzt man die Fragewörter who (wer) oder what (was) am Anfang, und setzt das Verb an die zweite Stelle.

Beispiele:

Who is your English teacher?	Wer ist dein Englischlehrer?
What is the answer?	Was ist die Antwort?

1 Read the answers and write the questions in your excercise book.
Lies die Antworten und schreibe die Fragen in dein Heft. Benutze KEINE Fragewörter.

1. ______ ? Yes, I can play tennis.
2. ______ ? No, Peter doesn't like Arsenal.
3. ______ ? Yes, my parents sometimes go to the cinema at the weekends.
4. ______ ? Yes, football is my hobby.
5. ______ ? No, we don't play hockey at school.
6. ______ ? Yes, I often watch TV in the evenings.

2 Ask in English.
Schreibe in dein Heft. Frage Robert auf Englisch, ob ...

1. Tim schnell rennen kann.
2. Tim einen Fußball hat.
3. Tims Freund Golf spielt.
4. Tim in einer Mannschaft spielt.

REMEMBER **Fragen mit Fragewörtern**

Bei Fragen, die mit Fragewörtern gebildet sind, stehen diese am Anfang des Fragesatzes.
Fragen mit Fragewörtern werden mit einer Form von to be oder mit einem Hilfsverb gebildet.
Wenn keine Form von to be und kein Hilfsverb im Satz stehen, muss do/does auf das Fragewort folgen.

Die Fragewörter sind:
What? = Was?
Who? = Wer? oder Wen?

When? = Wann?
Where? = Wo?
How? = Wie?
How long? = Wie lange?
Why? = Warum?

3 Make questions.

Bilde Fragen. In den unterstrichenen Satzteilen steht, wonach du fragen sollst. Schreibe die Fragen in dein Heft.

1. Tim plays football every Saturday.
2. The team plays in the gym.
3. Tim goes to the gym on his bike.
4. It takes 20 minutes to get to the gym.
5. The football practice starts at 4 o'clock.
6. At the weekend Tim plays football with his friends.
7. Tim's father is a professional footballer.
8. His father is never at home because he plays for an Italian team.
9. Tim often sees his father on television.
10. He is not happy when his father's team loses.

4 Ask in English.

Schreibe in dein Heft. Frage auf Englisch, ...

1. wann das Spiel anfängt.
2. wer heute spielt. (**Vorsicht!** Hier wird das *present progressive* gebraucht.)
3. wie lang die Halbzeit (= the break) ist.
4. warum die Spieler unterschiedliche Farben tragen.
5. wie du weißt, wann jemand ein Tor schießt (= score a goal).
6. wohin die Spieler in der Halbzeit gehen.
7. ob die Spieler ihre Fußballhemden waschen müssen.
8. wie die Spieler wissen, wann das Spiel vorbei ist.

REMEMBER Langformen – Kurzformen

Beim Sprechen verwendet man **Kurzformen**.
Bei den Kurzformen wird ein Buchstabe weggelassen. Er wird durch ein Apostroph oder Auslassungszeichen (') ersetzt.

Kurzformen gibt es bei den Verben be und have:

am/are/is	have/has
I am → I'm	I have → I've
you are → you're	you have → you've

Vorsicht! He is → he's (z. B. *He's in the bedroom*.). He has → he's (z. B. *He's got a dog*.). Du musst auf den Sinn achten, um die Bedeutung zu verstehen.

Auch bei der **Verneinung** gibt es Kurzformen. Hier wird not zu -n't und mit dem Verb zusammengeschrieben:

you are not → you aren't	you have not → you haven't
he is not → he isn't	he has not → he hasn't

Aber: I am not → I'm not

Weitere wichtige Kurzformen:

here is → here's	that is → that's	there is → there's
What is? → What's?	Who is? → Who's?	Where is? → Where's?

1 Underline the shortened forms in the text.
Unterstreiche die Kurzformen in diesem Text.

It's Saturday afternoon and Tim and Robert are waiting for their friends. They want to go to the beach on their bikes. "Where's the orange juice?" asks Tim. "Robert, there's no orange juice." "Yes, there is," says Robert. "Look, here's a bottle in my rucksack. But have you got the tennis balls?" "Yes, I've got Sally's tennis ball. My tennis ball is on the roof of the school," says Tim. "Well, I hope she is OK with that. She wants to play tennis this afternoon with her friends, too." "Yes, she's cool about it. She has a lot of balls. You know she's in a club," says Tim. "Hey, there's Paul. But where's Peter? He's late as usual!" says Robert.

2 Use the shortened forms.
Benutze die Kurzform. Schreibe deine Sätze in dein Heft.

1. Peter is a good basketball player.
2. He is in a team.
3. He has always got his basketball with him.
4. Look, Peter's team is playing now.
5. "We are winning," says Peter.
6. "You are playing very good basketball today," says Mr Green, the trainer, in the break.
7. But what is this? The other team has got the ball.
8. Oh, the other team is winning now.

3 Use the long forms.
Benutze die Langform. Schreibe in dein Heft.

1. My mother's a tennis player.
2. We don't play hockey in our school.
3. Sarah's brother's good at hockey.
4. My friend's got a basketball basket in his garden.
5. He's good at basketball.
6. There's a basketball team at his school.
7. Your favourite sport is sleeping and you're good at it!
8. Where's Paul's dog? It's always hiding.

1.3 Wortart: Pronomen

REMEMBER Die Personalpronomen

Man benutzt Pronomen (Begleiter), um eintöniges Wiederholen von Namen zu vermeiden.

Beispiel: Tom is my friend. Tom is 11 years old. Tom is in my class.
Besser: Tom is my friend. He is 11 years old. He is in my class.

Hier ist eine Übersicht:

Personalpronomen (Subjekt)	Personalpronomen (Objekt)
I	me
you	you
he	him
she	her
it	it
we	us
you	you
they	them

Aufpassen: Im Englischen verwendet man im Singular bei **Personen** he oder she. Für **alles andere** muss man it verwenden (mit Ausnahmen von Haustieren, deren Namen und Geschlecht man kennt. Hier kann man he oder she verwenden. Aber, nicht vergessen, in allen anderen Fällen muss man it verwenden.)

1 Replace the underlined words with the right personal pronoun.
Ersetze die unterstrichenen Wörter durch Personalpronomen.
Schreibe die entsprechenden Pronomen auf.

1. Peter goes climbing at the weekends. ______
2. His friends, Jack and Tom, like kayaking. ______
3. Peter sometimes goes with Jack and Tom. ______
4. His sister, Jane, sometimes goes, too. ______
5. Jack likes Jane. ______
6. And Jane likes Jack and Tom. ______
7. "Jane, you and I can go kayaking," says Jack. ______
8. The children look at Peter. ______
9. Peter looks at the boys and his sister and laughs. ______
10. Then he jumps into the kayak. ______

2 Fill in the missing pronouns.
Trage die fehlenden Pronomen ein.

Linda meets the girls. ______ are in the shop. Linda is talking to ______ . ______ are telling ______ that ______ are looking for a present for Robert. It is his birthday on Saturday. But ______ don't know what to buy ______. Linda says that ______ thinks a CD is a good present but the girls say ______ don't want to buy a CD. ______ think that ______ is too expensive. Suddenly Robert comes into the shop. "______ know that ______ are talking about my birthday," ______ says. "______ don't know what to buy ______ for my birthday!" Then Robert tells ______ what ______ wants. "Well, ______ don't want a CD. What

_______ want is a new golf ball. Golf is my new hobby. I like _______," _______ says.

"Do _______ know how much golf balls cost? _______ are very expensive," says Linda. "Well," says Robert, "_______ don't have to buy the expensive balls. _______ often lose balls when _______ play. Anyway, are _______ coming to my party on Saturday? _______ starts at 7 o'clock and _______ will be fun."

"Yes, great," say the girls. "_______ will all be there."

REMEMBER **Direkte und indirekte Aufforderungen**

Possessivpronomen werden verwendet, um auszudrücken, wem etwas gehört.
Hier ist eine Übersicht:

Personalpronomen (Subjekt)	Possessivpronomen (-begleiter)
I	my
you	your
he	his
she	her
it	its
we	our
you	your
they	their

Aufpassen: Bei folgenden Wörtern besteht Verwechslungsgefahr:
your (dein) → you're (you are = du bist)
its (sein) → it's (it is = es ist)
their (ihr) → they're (they are = sie sind) → there (dort)

3 Fill in the missing possessives.

Trage die fehlenden Possessivbegleiter ein.

Mandy is going to play basketball with her friend, David. He is in her class. their English teacher is there, too. He has got his dog with him. "Hello, Mr Martin," says Mandy. "Is that your dog?" "Yes, it is my dog. He is only three months old. His name is Gus."

Mandy and David talk to Mr Martin about his dog and then they start to play basketball with the other children. They are in the same team but their team is not very good. "Our team is going to lose," says Mandy. "We always lose!"

4 Say it in English.

Schreibe in dein Heft. Sage auf Englisch, dass ...

1. die Kinder ihre Hunde füttern.
2. du deine Schlange magst.
3. das Mädchen ihr Kaninchen in den Käfig setzt.
4. ihr eure Haustiere morgen in die Schule mitnehmen könnt.
5. unsere Katze 14 Jahre alt ist.

5 Possessives are better.

Verwende die Possessivbegleiter, um die Sätze zu verbessern.
Schreibe in dein Heft.

1. Patrick and Patrick's mother are in town.
2. The children and the children's parents want to go to the cinema.
3. Leonard and Laurence, the twins, and the twins' dog are in the garden.
4. They are playing with the dog and the dog's ball.
5. Hey, Tina, can I have Tina's phone number? Then I can phone you.

6 Tick ✓ the correct pronoun.

Setze einen Haken ✓ hinter das richtige Pronomen.

A: Tim is making a lot of noise!

B: I can ask ______ to be quiet.

a. him ☐ b. it ☐ c. its ☐

A: Please tell Janet to come here.

B: Sorry, I don't know ______.

a. her ☐ b. him ☐ c. she ☐

A: I can't find my pencils!

B: You are holding ______ in your hand!

a. them ☐ b. there ☐ c. they ☐

A: Do you like bananas?

B: I love ______.

a. hers ☐ b. its ☐ c. them ☐

A: Why is he always talking about Ms Jones, his English teacher?

B: I think he likes ______.

a. her ☐ b. him ☐ c. she ☐

A: Where is my book? Oh, dear! I've lost ______!

a. him ☐ b. it ☐ c. its ☐

A: I know your parents. I often see ______ at the supermarket on Saturday.

a. them b. there c. the

A: Is that Mary's new bike?

B: Don't ask me, ask ________.

a. her b. his c. it

A: Why is David so happy?

B: His friends gave ________ a guitar for his birthday.

a. him b. it c. them

A: Is she writing a letter to Peter?

B: Yes, she is in love with ________ !

a. her b. him c. his

A: What is the name of that book?

B: I'm sorry I can't remember ________ .

a. him b. it c. them

A: What are you going to do with those old papers?

B: I'm going to put ________ in the bin.

a. their b. them c. they

A: Let's see the new Harry Potter film.

B: No, I don't want to see ________ . I want to see Shrek.

a. him b. it c. there

1.4 Mengenbezeichnungen: *some* und *any*

REMEMBER Aussagen: *Some or any?*

In **bejahten Sätzen** verwendet man some (einige/ein paar/etwas).

Beispiele: My mum always gives me some fruit for school. – Meine Mutter gibt mir immer etwas Obst mit in die Schule.

I have some apples in my bag. Do you want one? – Ich habe ein paar Äpfel in meine Tasche. Möchtest du einen?

In **verneinten Sätzen** und in Fragen verwendest du any (einige/ein paar/etwas).

Beispiele: I haven't got any bread. – Ich habe kein Brot.

I haven't got any apples. – Ich habe keine Äpfel.

Beachte: Bei der Verneinung muss im Englischen immer **not** stehen (im Deutschen ist die Verneinung schon im Wort *kein* enthalten).

1 **Look at the picture and finish the sentences. Use *some* or *any*.**
Schau dir das Bild an und formuliere passende Sätze. Verwende *some* oder *any*.

EXAMPLE

(boys) *There are some boys.*
(cars) *There aren't any cars.*

1. (girls) *There ...*
2. (dogs)
3. (men)
4. (birds)
5. (ducks)
6. (buses)
7. (bikes)
8. (trees)
9. (babies)
10. (cats)

GOOD TO KNOW **Fragen: *Some or any?***

In Fragen verwendet man im Englischen normalerweise any, im Deutschen dagegen verwendet man *etwas* (in der Einzahl) bzw. *einige* oder *ein paar* (in der Mehrzahl).

Beispiele: Have you got any bread? – Hast du etwas Brot?
Have you got any apples? – Hast du ein paar Äpfel?

2 Read the text and fill in *some* or *any* in the gaps.
Lies den Text und ergänze mit *some* oder *any*.

Robert: Hi, grandma, what is your new flat like?

Grandma: It's nice. There is a big road outside my flat. And there is a lot to see when I look out of my windows. From the living room window I can usually see ______ cars and lots of lorries. But it is Sunday today so I can't see ______ lorries. There are ______ people on their bikes. There are ______ new bikes and ______ old bikes but there aren't ______ mountain bikes today.

Robert: What about your bedroom window? Can you see ______ cars or lorries from that window?

Grandma: No, I can see the park from my bedroom window. So I can often see ______ dogs and ______ children but I can't see ______ rabbits. And I can't see ______ cars or lorries or taxis.

3 Some or any?

Entscheide, ob du *some* oder *any* einsetzen musst. Schreibe das richtige Wort auf.

1. Mandy is going to the cinema with ______ of her friends.
2. Jane doesn't have ______ friends.
3. Have you got ______ brothers or sisters?
4. Here is ______ food for your picnic in the park.
5. Are there ______ postcards of our town in that shop?
6. I'm hungry. Have we got ______ apples? No, sorry, there aren't ______. I must buy ______ tomorrow at the supermarket.

4 Say it in English.

Schreibe in dein Heft.

1. Frage auf Englisch, ob es (irgendwelche) großen Schulen in dieser Stadt gibt.
2. Sage auf Englisch, dass du einige Freunde in deiner Straße hast.
3. Sage auf Englisch, dass in deiner Straße einige große Autos parken.
4. Frage auf Englisch, ob es in deiner Stadt (irgendwelche) Kinos gibt.
5. Sage auf Englisch, dass du kein Geld hast.

5 Fill in *some* or *any*.
Setze *some* oder *any* ein.

1. Only ______ of Jack's friends are at the party. Not all of them.
2. A: There isn't ______ cheese in the kitchen.
   B: I can buy ______ bread and ______ cheese at the supermarket this afternoon.
4. We don't have ______ chocolate to make a chocolate cake.
5. Don't close the door. There are still ______ children outside.
6. Let's put ______ white flowers on the table.
7. I have so much homework. I haven't got ______ time to talk with you now.
8. ______ people like to work in the morning; other people like to work at night.
9. Have you got ______ questions about the test?
10. There aren't ______ books about horses in the library.
11. ______ books about camping can help you put up a tent.
12. Mia gave Robert ______ help with his homework, so he is very happy.
13. The teacher hasn't got ______ time to correct the tests now. She can do it at the weekend.
14. I have ______ dictionaries in my room that you can use.
15. Here are ______ nice red apples.

1.5 Genitiv-s

REMEMBER **Verwendung des Genitiv-s**

Man benutzt ein Apostroph + s ('s) oder ein s + Apostroph (s'), um zu zeigen, dass jemandem etwas gehört.

Beispiel: Mary's children are loud. – Es sind Marys Kinder. Das erkennt man an dem 's.
Jenny's dog is big. – Der Hund gehört Jenny. Auch das erkennt man am 's. Auf Deutsch sagt man „Jennys Hund".

Endet ein Name einer Person oder z. B. einer Straße mit einem s, so schreibt man üblicherweise auch ein 's am Ende des Namens.

Beispiel: Mr Jones's dog is running down St. James's Street. Charles's Mum doesn't like that.

Falls das Wort aber für eine Gruppe von Leuten oder eine Gruppe von Sachen steht und es ein s am Ende hat, hängt man ein Apostroph hinter das s. Aber <u>nur</u> dann, wenn man ausdrücken möchte, dass jemandem etwas gehört!

Beispiel: The Browns' children are very nice. Gemeint sind die Kinder der Familie Brown. Da es sich um mehrere Personen handelt, spricht man von den Browns (Plural).
Here are the five teams' results.
Those two dogs' tails are wagging.
All those cars' lights are on. – Let's put our lights on.

Bei zwei Personen wird nur einmal 's angehängt.

Beispiel: Tim and Robert's grandmother is a teacher.

Bei allen Wörtern, die zwar in der Mehrzahl stehen, aber kein s am Ende haben, wie z. B. children oder men wird nur ein 's angehängt.

Beispiel: The children's bikes are there. The men's cars are dirty.

1 Write the names in the gaps. Where does the apostrophe go?
Schreibe die Namen in die Lücken hinein. Entscheide, wo du das Apostroph setzen musst.

1. I know ________ sister. (Mandy)
2. This is ________ house. (Peter)
3. Let's go to the ________ (Smiths) house. They are our new neighbours.
4. The ________ room is upstairs. (children)
5. ________ house is two hundred years old. (John)
6. In this shop ________ shoes are on the second floor. (men)
7. ________ and ________ bikes have got blue stickers. (Robert - Tim)
8. My ________ car wasn't expensive. (parents)
   ________ ________ car is new. (Charles – father)
9. The football ________ trainer is very good. (team)
10. My ________ house is next to our house. (friend)
11. The ________ basket and the ________ basket are in the kitchen. (dog – cats)
12. ________ desk is next to ________ desk. (Jonas – Michael)

2 Say it in English.
Schreibe in dein Heft. Sage, dass ...

1. das Auto deines Englischlehrers vor der Bibliothek ist.
2. der Freund deines Bruders neben euch wohnt.
3. die Mutter deiner Freundin in Afrika ist.
4. der Hund deiner Eltern dich nicht mag.
5. das Haus deiner Nachbarn groß ist.

1.6 *This, that, these, those*

REMEMBER Verwendung

This (Singular) und these (Plural) verwendet man bei Dingen, die sich in der Nähe befinden.
That (Singular) und those (Plural) verwenden wir bei weiter entfernten Dingen.

Beispiele:

David: Can you give me that book from the table over there?
Frank: This book here?
David: Yes, that one.
Frank: Here you are. Oh, can you also give me those magazines from that other table over there, please?
David: These magazines? Yes, of course, here you are.

Hier ist eine Übersicht:

	this	**that**
Singular	*This is a book in my hand.*	*That is his car over there.*
	these	**those**
Plural	*These are my friends sitting next to me.*	*Those girls over there are my sisters.*
	etwas ist näher dran	etwas ist weiter weg (zeitlich und örtlich)

1 Fill in the right form – singular or plural.
Schreibe die jeweils die fehlende Form – Singular oder Plural – dazu.

1. this car, ________ cars
2. ________ boy, those boys
3. that girl, ________ girls
4. ________ child, these children

5. ________ banana, these bananas
6. this town, ________ towns
7. ________ school, those schools
8. that teacher, ________ teachers

2 Fill in *this, that, these* or *those.*

Ergänze *this, that, these* oder *those*. Schreibe in die Lücken.

1. Can you give me ________ pencil over there, please?
2. ________ dolls on the table here are very old.
3. Can you see ________ building next to the bank? It is my new school.
4. ________ bus here does not go to town. You need ________ bus over there, the 44.
5. Susan: Look at ________ bike over here. It's great. You need a new bike, Gordon.
6. Gordon: Yes, but it is too expensive. ________ bike over there is not expensive.
7. Susan: Let's go over the road to "Bikes and More". ________ bikes are good, and fast, too.
8. Gordon: I don't want a fast bike. ________ bikes here are OK for me. I think I will buy ________ green bike in the shop window over there next to the black bike. It looks good.
9. Susan: No, don't bother with ________ bikes. They are NOT good. The bikes in ________ shop are really NOT good. Come with me to ________ shop over there. I know the bikes there are good. My brother always buys his bikes in ________ shop.

3 Write some sentences about things in your room using *this, that, these, those.*

Schreibe einige Sätze, in denen du *this*, *that*, *these* und *those* verwendest.

4 Say it in English.

Schreibe in dein Heft. Sage auf Englisch, dass ...

1. die Bücher hier englisch sind und die Bücher dort deutsch sind.
2. die Jungen dort drüben deine Freunde sind.
3. die Bleistifte dort neu sind und der Füller hier auch.
4. das Fahrrad hier deiner Schwester gehört.
5. Petra in dem Haus dort drüben wohnt. Die Häuser dort neu sind.
6. diese Socken nicht deine sind.
7. du viele Bücher hast, aber diese zwei deine Lieblingsbücher sind.

5 Put in *this, that, these* or *those.*

Ergänze *this, that, these* oder *those.*

1. Look over there! I think ______ is the biggest car in the world.
2. Miriam told me ______ joke about the spider yesterday.
3. Matthew, take ______ book and put it over there, please.
4. Melanie, come and look at ______ oranges. Some of them are bad.
5. Look at ______ elephants sleeping under the tree over there.
6. I think ______ is the best day of my life.
7. Did you see ______ pupils in the office? They want to come to our school.
8. Let's watch the plane flying through ______ big cloud.
9. ______ film Dad always talks about sounds interesting.

1.7 Die modalen Hilfsverben *can* und *must, mustn't, needn't*

REMEMBER Verwendung

Mit must wird im Englischen ausgedrückt, dass man etwas tun muss.
Beispiel: The boy must do his homework. Der Junge muss seine Hausaufgaben machen.
I must give the rabbit some food. Ich muss dem Kaninchen etwas Futter geben.

Mustn't bedeutet „nicht dürfen". Mit mustn't (= must not) wird ausgedrückt, dass etwas verboten ist.
Beispiel: You **mustn't** cross the road when the lights are red. Du **darfst** die Strasse **nicht** überqueren, wenn die Ampel rot ist.

Achtung Verwechslungsgefahr! Das englische **mustn't** (= darf nicht) und das deutsche „müssen nicht" (man braucht nicht) sind zwei Wortgruppen, die nichts miteinander zu tun haben!

Mit needn't (Langform: need not) wird ausgedrückt, dass jemand etwas nicht tun muss.

Beispiel: You **needn't** make any sandwiches. I can buy some at the supermarket.

1 **Match the words on the left with the German phrases on the right.**
Kombiniere die englischen Wörter auf der linken Seite mit den deutschen auf der rechten Seite. Verbinde die jeweiligen Wörter mit einem Strich.

must	*kann*
mustn't	*kann nicht*
needn't	*muss nicht / braucht nicht*
can	*muss*
can't	*darf nicht*

2 Fill in the gaps with *must*, *can* or *can't*.
Schreibe *must*, *can* oder *can't* in die Lücken.

1. Paul: "Mum, ______ I go out and play football with my friends?" Mother: "No, you ______ . You ______ do your homework first."
2. The doctor says you ______ stay in bed because you are sick (= krank).
3. They ______ run to get the bus. I can see it at the corner.
4. John, ______ you play the piano? – Yes, I ______ play the piano and I ______ play the trumpet.
5. You ______ do your homework at home, not on the bus.
6. It is warm enough today so we ______ swim in the swimming pool in the garden.
7. "Mrs Dickson, ______ I sit here next to my friend, Molly?" "Yes, Carol, you ______ sit there."
8. "Mum, ______ I watch TV?" "No, Tim, you ______ , your father is sleeping."
9. Doris ______ walk now because she is 18 months old.
10. "Dad, ______ I go to the cinema?" – "Yes, you ______ but you ______ be home before ten."

3 Choose the right modal verb.
Wähle das richtige modale Hilfsverb für die Sätze. Schreibe sie in die Lücken.

1. Today I __________ (cannot / mustn't) go to school, because I am sick. The doctor says I __________ (mustn't / needn't) get out of bed but that I __________ (needn't / mustn't) sleep.
2. The children __________ (must / can) clean up their rooms this morning.
3. I __________ (can / can't) go to bed late tomorrow evening because it is Friday.
4. __________ I eat (must / can) lunch at my friend's house tomorrow?
5. The boys __________ (mustn't / can) eat all that fruit today. I'm going to buy new fruit tomorrow anyway.
6. Jenny __________ (can / must) go to the disco this Friday.

1.8 Wortstellung im Satz

REMEMBER **Satzstellung S – V – O**

Im Englischen muss immer eine bestimmte Reihenfolge der Satzteile eingehalten werden. Diese Reihenfolge ist:

Subjekt – Verb – Objekt
(**S**traßen**V**erkehrs**O**rdnung / SVO)

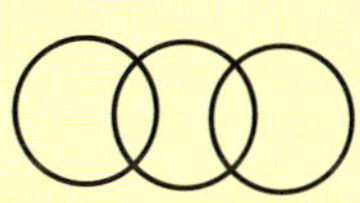

Verb und Objekt gehören zusammen und man darf keine anderen Satzteile dazwischen stellen.

1 Rearrange the words and phrases into a proper sentence.

Bringe die Satzteile in die richtige Reihenfolge. Schreibe die Sätze in dein Heft.

1. *and* *Colin* *in town* *Tammy* *are*
2. *a new coat* *Tammy* *wants* .
3. *hates* *Colin* *shopping* *going* .
4. *they* *now* *shop* *are* *a big* *in* .
5. *is trying on* *Tammy* *a new coat*
6. *not happy* *is* *Colin* .
7. *model cars* *he* *some* *is looking at* .
8. *Tammy* *forgets* *he* .

REMEMBER **Adverbien des Ortes und der Zeit**

Ortsangaben und Zeitangaben stehen meist am Satzende. Sie stehen **nie** zwischen Verb und Objekt. Kommen in einem Satz Orts- und Zeitangaben vor, dann gilt: **O**rt vor **Z**eit (O vor Z, wie im Alphabet).

2 Say it in English.

Schreibe in dein Heft. Sage auf Englisch, dass ...

1. Andy am Mittwochnachmittag in der Schule Bingo spielt.
2. Laura freitagabends in der Disco Karaoke singt.
3. die Jungen nachmittags im Park Fußball spielen.
4. Mr Green im Sommer in England Fotos macht.
5. Johns Mutter dienstags in der Bücherei Deutsch lernt.

Test

1 Make questions.

Bilde Fragen. In den unterstrichenen Satzteilen steht, wonach du fragen sollst. Schreibe die Fragen in dein Heft.

1. I am just going to <u>get ready</u>. *What ...*
2. The bus is going to come <u>in 10 minutes.</u>
3. We are going to buy the tickets <u>on the bus</u>.
4. Bob is going to pay for <u>the tickets</u> with his money.
5. <u>Dad and Mum</u> are going to come with us.

2 Write the names in the gaps. Where does the apostrophe go?

Schreibe die Namen in die Lücken.
Entscheide, wo du das Apostroph setzen musst.

1. My ______ bike is broken. (brother)
2. ______ bike is red. (Simon)
3. My ______ parents are all very nice. (friends)
4. The ______ bikes are at school. (children)
5. My ______ computer is very fast. (sister)

3 Put the parts of the sentences in the right order.

Bringe die Satzteile in die richtige Reihenfolge.
Schreibe die Sätze in dein Heft.

1. *is going to* | *her mother* | *this Saturday* | *Linda* | *to help* | *in the garden*
2. *sometimes* | *with her friends* | *at the weekend* | *to town* | *goes* | *she*
3. *but* | *on holiday* | *all her friends* | *are*

2 Texte verstehen

Das musst du am Ende der Klasse 5 können:

im Bereich Lesen und verstehen:

- ▷ Kurze, einfach Texte lesen
- ▷ Gezielt Informationen im Text finden
- ▷ Kurze, persönliche Briefe verstehen
- ▷ Einen Text so gut verstehen, dass du falsche Aussagen zum Inhalt bemerkst

im Bereich Hören und verstehen:

- ▷ Alltägliche Ausdrücke und einfache Sätze - z. B. kurze einfache Anweisungen - verstehen, wenn deutlich und langsam gesprochen wird
- ▷ Einzelheiten in einem Hörtext mithilfe von Bildern verstehen
- ▷ Einen Hörtext so genau verstehen, dass du sagen kannst, welche Aussagen richtig und welche falsch sind

2.1 Lesen und verstehen

GOOD TO KNOW **Richtig lesen**

Auch wenn dir ein Text im ersten Moment schwierig vorkommt: Wenn du Schritt für Schritt vorgehst, wirst du ihn besser verstehen.

- ▶ Bevor du einen Text liest, frage dich, was die **Überschrift** bedeuten könnte. Sie kann dir einige Tipps zum Inhalt geben.
- ▶ Lies den ganzen Text durch und versuche zunächst, **unbekannte Wörter** aus dem Zusammenhang zu verstehen.
- ▶ Beim zweiten Lesen suche die wichtigsten **Schlüsselwörter** heraus.

Du sollst zeigen, dass du den Text verstanden hast. So gehst du vor:

- ▶ Lies die Aufgabenstellung sorgfältig durch.
- ▶ Suche die passende Textstelle im Text.
- ▶ Lies die Stelle im Text **und** die Aufgabenstellung noch einmal sorgfältig durch - dann löse die Aufgabe.

A familiy tree

Peter is married to Susan. She is his wife and he is her husband. They have a daughter and a son. The son's name is Mark and the daughter's name is Linda. They live next to Susan's parents, Harry and Sharon. Harry is Susan's father and Sharon is her mother. Mark is Harry's grandson and Linda is Sharon's granddaughter. Susan has a sister and a brother. Her sister's name is Mary and her brother's name is Patrick. Patrick has two children, David and Samantha. Susan is their aunt and Peter is their uncle.

1 Complete the following using the opposite family members. The first has been done for you.
Vervollständige die folgende Tabelle und ergänze die passenden Familienmitglieder. Das erste Beispiel ist schon fertig.

husband	wife
son	
	aunt
	sister
grandfather	
	granddaughter
father	

2 Answer these questions.
Beantworte die Fragen.

1. What is the name of Peter's son?
2. Who is Linda's grandfather?
3. And who is Mark's uncle?
4. What is the name of Susan's mother?

3 There are 14 words in the puzzle. Find them.
They are hidden in these directions: → ↓ ↗ ↘ ↙
In diesem Suchrätsel sind 14 Wörter versteckt. Finde sie.
Sie sind in folgende Richtungen versteckt: → ↓ ↗ ↘ ↙.

Die gesuchten Wörter sind die englischen Begriffe für:

1. *Enkelin* 2. *Kinder* 3. *Enkel* 4. *Tochter*
5. *Eltern* 6. *Bruder* 7. *Ehemann* 8. *Schwester*
9. *Mutter* 10. *Vater* 11. *Onkel*
12. *Tante* 13. *Ehefrau* 14. *Sohn*

Q	K	M	N	S	I	S	T	E	R	K	S	I
Q	F	O	F	A	T	H	E	R	E	P	P	C
L	S	T	X	G	G	U	J	H	X	A	Q	Q
L	C	H	O	R	S	X	N	V	A	R	O	X
L	R	E	N	A	N	E	M	J	T	E	K	H
B	G	R	Z	N	R	H	B	N	K	N	J	M
G	R	A	N	D	D	A	U	G	H	T	E	R
E	M	G	L	S	Q	A	O	S	E	S	Y	R
N	K	I	C	O	U	L	T	P	B	V	A	E
F	H	B	U	N	C	L	E	C	I	A	F	D
C	A	D	A	U	G	H	T	E	R	I	N	N
B	R	O	T	H	E	R	R	O	W	V	C	D

4 Write a text about your family in your exercise book.
Schreibe einen Text über deine Familie.

Two sisters and the cat

Mrs Black and Mrs Jackson are sisters. Mrs Black lives in a house in Dundee and Mrs Jackson lives in a flat in Glasgow. One day Mrs Black visits her sister. When Mrs Jackson opens the door she is crying[1]. “What’s the matter?” Mrs Black asks. Her sister says “My old cat Sammy died[2] last night but where can I bury[3] him?”
Mrs Black is unhappy because she knows that her sister loves the cat. Then she says “I can bury your cat in my garden in Dundee and you can come and visit him.” Mrs. Jackson stops crying and the two sisters have a cup of tea.
It is now five o’clock and Mrs Black wants to go home. She fetches her jacket and Mrs Jackson puts the cat into a shopping bag. Mrs Black takes the shopping bag and walks to the bus stop. She buys a magazine. When the bus comes she gets on[4] the bus, sits down and puts the shopping bag on the floor next to her. She then begins to read the magazine. After two hours she gets off[5] the bus. She walks home.
When she gets home she says: “Oh, no, the shopping bag is still on the bus.”

[1] to cry = weinen
[2] died (to die) = starb
[3] to bury = begraben
[4] to get on = einsteigen
[5] to get off = aussteigen

You can also listen to the CD. Track 1

1 Find the right answer.
Finde die richtige Antwort. Mache einen Haken (✓) in das richtige Kästchen.

1. Where does Mrs Black live? She lives in …
   - a flat in Dundee.
   - a flat in Glasgow.
   - a house in Dundee.

2. Why is Mrs Jackson unhappy? She is unhappy because …
   - her sister wants to see her cat.
   - her sister died.
   - her cat died.

3. What does Mrs Black do?
- X ☐ She takes the cat with her on the bus.
- ☐ She puts her magazine in the shopping bag.
- ☐ She makes tea for her sister.

4. How does Mrs Black go home?
- ☐ She walks.
- X ☐ She goes by bus.
- ☐ She goes by car.

5. When does Mrs Black get home? She gets home ...
- ☐ after 9 p.m.
- X ☐ after 7 p.m.
- ☐ after 7 a.m.

6. When does Mrs Black remember Sammy? She remembers Sammy ...
- X ☐ when she gets home.
- ☐ when she gets off the bus.
- ☐ when she gets on the bus.

2 Find the words for these definitions. They are all in the text.

Schreibe die richtigen Begriffe für die folgenden Erklärungen hinter die Sätze. Sie stehen alle im Text.

1. She is your mother's daughter. ____________
2. This is a place to live and it usually has a garden. ____________
3. You are this when you get a bad mark in a test. ____________
4. When a person or an animal dies, you ____________ them.
5. The teacher ____________ a question and wants an answer.

3 Write definitions for these words.

Schreibe englische Erklärungen für die folgenden Begriffe auf.

bus stop *shopping bag* *magazine*

4 All these words have double letters. Fill in the missing letters.
Diese Wörter werden mit doppelten Buchstaben geschrieben. Ergänze die fehlenden Buchstaben.

d ___ r   f ___ t   ha ___ y   ma ___ er

sho ___ ing   sti ___   su ___ enly

5 All these words have two vowels together. Fill in the missing letters.
Diese Wörter werden mit Doppelvokalen geschrieben. Ergänze die fehlenden Buchstaben.

bec ___ se   h ___ rs   h ___ se   r ___ d   t ___

Rover, a very cold dog

The Walkers have got a dog. His name is Rover. Rover lives in a dog kennel[1] in the garden. This is OK in the summer but now it's winter, and Rover is cold[2]. In his little house in the garden it's very cold. What can he do? He runs around the garden and sees the neighbours'[3] house. The front door is open.
He goes to the neighbours' door and into the hall. It's nice and warm in there. Then he runs into the kitchen. The kitchen is very big. Next he goes into the living room with the sofa and a big TV. On the TV there is a film about Africa and Rover watches it, but it's boring! Next he goes into the dining room[4]. There are six chairs and a table. Rover runs upstairs. Here are the parents' bedroom and the children's bedrooms. There are beds in them and they look very warm. But no, that's not what Rover wants. Behind the brown door there is a bathroom with a bath and a toilet. Rover doesn't stop here. He runs up to the attic[5]. There are a lot of old things here but nothing for Rover!
Rover goes back to the hall. Look, there is a long red scarf! That's it! Rover takes the scarf in his mouth[6] and runs back into his garden. Now the kennel is very nice and very warm. "That's better!" thinks Rover.

[1] kennel = Hundehütte
[2] cold = kalt
[3] neighbours = Nachbarn
[4] dining room = Esszimmer
[5] attic = Dachboden
[6] mouth = Mund, Maul

You can also listen to the CD. **Track 2**

1 True, false, not in the text? Put a tick (✓) in the right box.
Richtig, falsch oder gar nicht im Text? Setze einen Haken (✓) in das entsprechende Kästchen.

	true	false	not in the text
1. Rover is six months old.			
2. The kennel is in the Walkers' garden.			
3. Sometimes the kennel is OK.			
4. The neighbours are very nice.			
5. The neighbours' kitchen is big.			
6. The TV is in the kitchen.			
7. There are six chairs in the dining room.			
8. The neighbours have three children.			
9. There are more than two bedrooms.			
10. The bathroom has a black door.			
11. Rover takes a scarf from the hall.			

2 Now correct the sentences that are wrong.
Verbessere nun die falschen Aussagen in Aufgabe 1. Schreibe in dein Heft.

3 Find where Rover goes. Write the sentences in your exercise book.
Finde heraus, wohin Rover geht. Schreibe die Sätze mit den notwendigen Satzzeichen in dein Heft.

RoveriscoldHegoestotheneighboursfront doorandintothehallThenherunsintothe kitchenNexthegoesintothelivingroomRover runsupstairsHerearetheparents bedroomandthechildrensbedroomsThereisa bathroomHerunsuptotheatticThenhegoes backtothehallHerunsbackintohisgarden

4 Now number the rooms to show the path that Rover takes through the house.

Zeige Rovers Weg durch das Haus. Setze Zahlen in der richtigen Reihenfolge in den Zimmern ein.

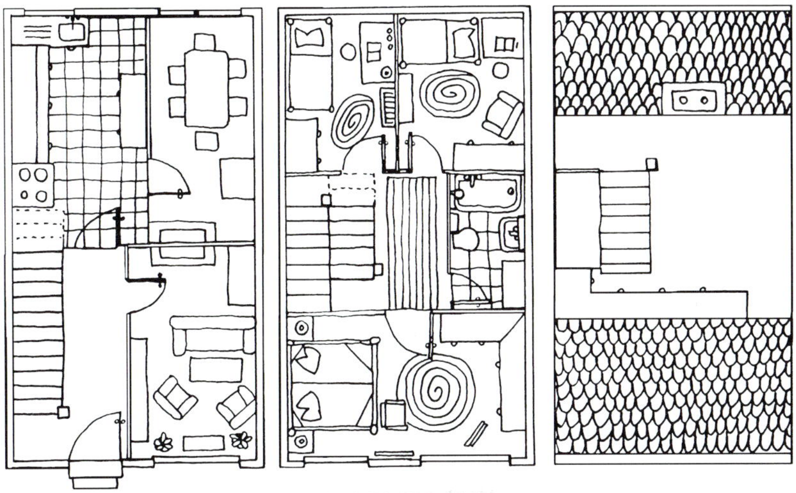

5 Say it in English.

Schreibe in dein Heft. Sage auf Englisch, dass ...

1. es im Winter sehr kalt ist.
2. die Tür offen ist.
3. er nach oben rennt.
4. es sehr warm aussieht.
5. es hier viele alte Sachen gibt.

Houses

1 Read about the families and find the right house for them.
Lies die Aussagen über die Familien und finde für jede das richtige Haus.

The Green family have got three children. There is Mary. She is seven, and her twin brothers, Tim and Robert, are two. Sometimes their grandmother comes and visits them.

Mr and Mrs Pretty have got a six month old daughter. Her name is Caitlyn. Sometimes Caitlyn's grandfather and grandmother visit them. Caitlyn's grandfather can paint and he can make things with wood.

The Brown family have two sons. One son, Max, is fifteen and the other son, Peter, is thirteen. Max is very good at sports and plays basketball in a team. He likes football and is good at inline skating. Peter loves books. He reads and plays chess.

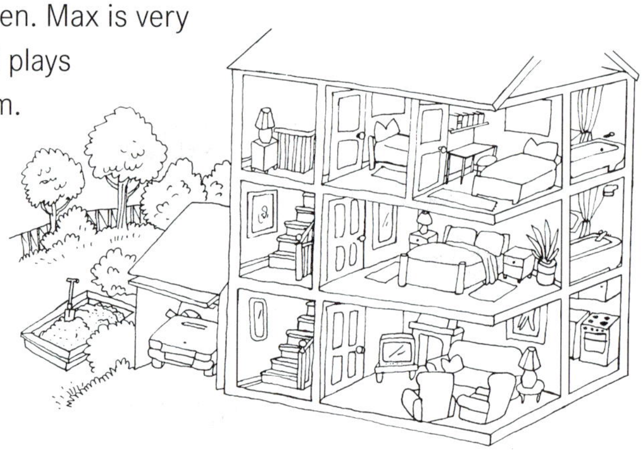

A.

B.

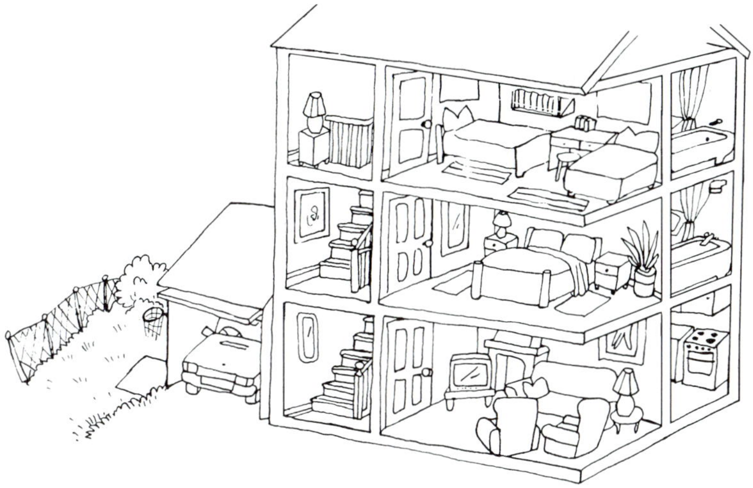

C.

D.

2 Which family?

Welche Familie? Lies die Fragen und entscheide, um welche Familie es sich handelt. (Es können manchmal zwei Familien sein.)

1. Which house has sometimes got 6 people in it?
2. Which family has got a sports person?
3. Which family has got somebody to make things?
4. Which family has a quiet person?
5. Which family needs a big garden?

The new car

Colin's father has a new car. It is very big, very fast, very expensive[1] and very beautiful.
Every weekend, Colin and his father wash the car. Colin's father parks it outside his house. He wants all the people in the street to see this beautiful car.
Colin loves to show his friends his father's car. His father only puts it in the garage when it is raining. Colin doesn't like rain because he wants all his friends to see the car. He wants them to say, "Oh Colin, your dad's got a great car," or "Oh Colin, that's a very fast car."
One day, Colin's father is standing outside his house. He is talking to some people about his car. Then it starts to rain.
"Oh no!" says his father, "It's raining. Wait a minute please!"
He runs inside the house. Where are the keys[2] to his garage? He can't find them. He looks outside. Terrible rain is falling on his car. He takes an umbrella[3] and runs back into the street.
"Why do you need the umbrella?" asked Colin
Colin's father laughs. "Silly boy, it's raining."
"But if you don't like the rain you can sit in your car."
Colin's father laughs. "No, Colin, the umbrella isn't for me. It's for my car."
His father opens his umbrella and stands in the rain. He holds the umbrella over his car. Soon he is very wet[4]. But the car's roof is dry[5]. More people come to watch.
"You see, Colin," says his father. "Everybody wants to see my new car. It is so big, so fast, so expensive and so beautiful."
"No, Dad," answers Colin. "They don't want to see your car. They want to see a wet man holding an umbrella over his car."

[1] expensive = teuer
[2] keys = Schlüssel
[3] umbrella = Regenschirm
[4] wet = nass
[5] dry = trocken

You can also listen to the CD. **Track 3**

1 Find the right answers.

Finde die richtigen Antworten. Setze einen Haken (✓) in das entsprechende Kästchen.

1. Colin's father washes his car ...
   - ☐ every week.
   - ☐ every month.
   - ☐ every day.

2. Colin's father parks his car outside because ...
   - ☐ he wants all the people to see him.
   - ☐ he wants all the people to see it.
   - ☐ he can't find the keys to the garage.

3. Colin loves to show his friends his father's new car because ...
   - ☐ he loves his friends.
   - ☐ he loves the car.
   - ☐ he loves his friends saying it is a great car.

4. When it starts to rain Colin's father is talking about ...
   - ☐ some people.
   - ☐ Colin.
   - ☐ his car.

5. Colin's father looks for the garage keys ...
   - ☐ in the garden.
   - ☐ in the house.
   - ☐ in the car.

6. Everybody wants to see ...
   - ☐ a wet man with an umbrella.
   - ☐ a man with a car.
   - ☐ a wet car and a wet man.

2 Find the opposite for these words. They are all in the text.
Finde die Gegensätze zu den folgenden Wörtern. Sie stehen alle im Text auf Seite 62. Schreibe sie in die Tabelle.

small	
slow	
inside	
loves	
stops	
great	
closes	
stand	

3 A crossword puzzle
Write the English words in the puzzle. They are all in the text. Now find the word. It tells you where Rover goes first.
Trage die englischen Wörter in das Kreuzworträtsel ein. Sie stehen alle im Text. Das Wort auf den unterlegten Feldern sagt dir, wohin Rover zuerst geht. Die Lösung besteht aus zwei Wörtern.

Answer: He goes to the neighbours' ______________ .

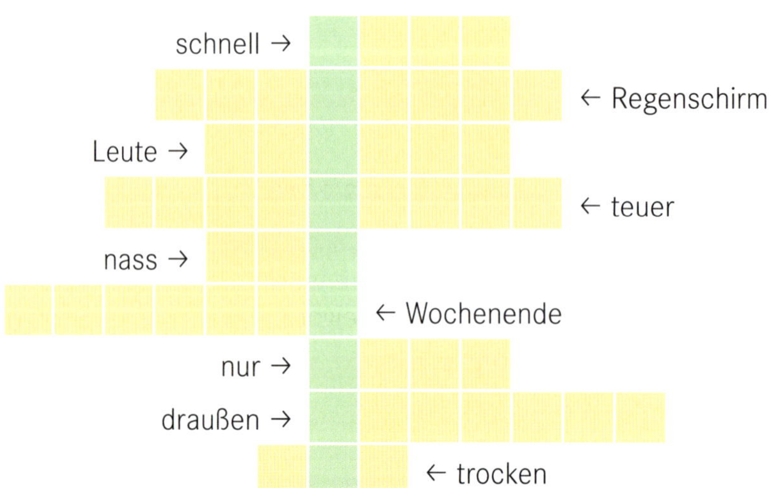

Two in one

1 **Here are two texts but they are mixed. Write the two texts in your exercise book.**
Hier sind zwei Texte durcheinander geraten. Markiere zunächst in zwei Farben, was zusammengehört. Schreibe die beiden Texte in dein Heft.

On school days I wake up at six o'clock. We have got a new house. It is a big white house with blue windows. I go to the bathroom and wash. There is a big garden with an apple tree where my four year old brother plays. Then I go to our very small kitchen for breakfast. My big sister, Susan, has muesli with milk or yoghurt. There is a garage for the car and our bikes and John's little scooter. She drinks a cup of tea. The living room and the kitchen are downstairs and they are very big. I have toast with butter and I drink a glass of milk. At seven o'clock we leave the house. Upstairs the rooms are small. There are three bedrooms and a bathroom. At the weekend we all have breakfast at eight o'clock. From my bedroom I can see the garden. Dad and I have bacon and eggs[1] and mum and Susan have a soft boiled egg[2]. Dad is a writer and he has got an office in the house. Everybody has orange juice and lots of toast. The office is the room next to John's bedroom.

[1] bacon and eggs = Speck und Eier

[2] soft boiled egg = weich gekochtes Ei

2 **What is each text about? Give it a title.**
Worum geht es in den beiden Texten? Finde Überschriften.

3 **Find ...**
Finde die gesuchten Begriffe und schreibe sie in dein Heft.

1. words that talk about time. (There are five.)
2. names of rooms. (There are five.)
3. names for other parts belonging to a house. (There are three.)
4. things to eat and drink. (There are eight.)

4 Which text is it? Write the name of the text (see exercise 2) behind each sentence.

Um welchen Text geht es? Schreibe die Überschrift (von Aufgabe 2) zu den Sätzen. Schreibe in dein Heft.

1. In this text the speaker goes to school. *That is ...*
2. In this text the speaker has a sister.
3. In this text the speaker's father is a writer.
4. In this text there are four rooms upstairs.
5. In this text the house has a small kitchen.
6. In this text the speaker has a brother.

My mum is funny

My mum is so funny. All my family say that she is funny. My family is my dad (he is 45 years old), my mum (she is 40 years old), my sister Molly (six years old), and me. I am ten years old. My name is Oscar. Oh, yes, and our small brown dog, Jacky. I don't know how old our dog is. My mum doesn't want to be funny. But she is. At the moment I am watching TV in the living room. My mother is in the living room, too. But now I can hear her. She is saying numbers: 15 and 89 and 72 and 45. I look at her. What is she doing? My mother is holding the TV remote control[1] in her hand. She is pressing the buttons[2] on it. She thinks it is a calculator.[3] I laugh and she looks at me. I tell her that it's not a calculator; it's the TV remote control. She laughs and gives it to me.

She is not funny all the time. But she is always different to other mums. My friends do not have a mum like my mum.

For example, what is she doing now? She is turning on the computer. The computer is also in the living room. It is the family computer. My mother is playing a computer game! But I want my dinner. I'm hungry and my sister is hungry, too.

[1] remote control = Fernbedienung
[2] buttons = Knöpfe
[3] calculator = Taschenrechner

"Mum, when is dinner?" I ask. "Not now, dear," she says. "I want to see how many Lemming levels I can play," is her answer. Lemming levels! I look at the computer and yes, my mother is playing Lemmings again! It's a computer game. It's not easy. You must save lemmings. "But, Mum, that computer game! You play it every day. And I am hungry," I say. "Yes, yes." is the answer I get. Not a good answer, I think. What can I do now? Turn off the computer? No! Shout? No! Phone a pizza restaurant? Good idea. So I phone a pizza restaurant and in thirty minutes my sister and I are eating pizza in the kitchen. Mum? She is still playing!

You can also listen to the CD. **Track 4**

1 Read the sentences. Put a tick (✓) in the right box.
Lies die folgenden Sätze. Setze einen Haken (✓) in das richtige Feld.

	true	false	not in the text
1. Oscar is eleven years old.			
2. Molly is in the first class at school.			
3. Oscar's mum has a job.			
4. Oscar's mum is funny.			
5. Oscar's mum thinks the pocket calculator is a TV remote control.			
6. Oscar's mum likes computer games.			
7. Oscar's mum is good at computer games.			
8. Oscar likes computer games.			
9. Oscar's sister is hungry.			
10. Oscar likes salami pizza.			

2 Write all the wrong sentences in your exercise book and make them right.
Schreibe die falschen Aussagen in dein Heft und korrigiere sie.

3 Who thinks this? Read the sentences and write *Oscar* or *his mother* after each sentence.
Wer denkt das? Lies die Sätze und schreibe *Oscar* oder *his mother* hinter jeden Satz.

1. Why is my mum different to my friends' mothers? That is ______.
2. I hope mum doesn't change my TV programme. That is ______.
3. Now where is that pocket calculator? That is ______.
4. Have we got enough money for pizzas? That is ______.
5. This is the ninth level – great! That is ______.
6. I can't cook. That is ______.
7. I'm hungry. That is ______.
8. I think Molly likes pizza. That is ______.

4 Put the sentences in the right order.
Schreibe die Sätze in der richtigen Reihenfolge auf.

She plays computer games every day.
Oscar has a funny mother.
When she plays computer games she forgets to make dinner.
She often does funny things.
Sometimes she uses the remote control to calculate.
She loves computer games.
Then Oscar gets pizza from a pizza restaurant.

5 Oscar writes an email to his grandmother. He tells her about his mother and computer games.
Schreibe Oscars E-Mail an seine Großmutter. Erzähle ihr von seiner Mutter und von Computerspielen.

Test

Max

A. Max is nine years old and lives near a river in a very big house. He has a very big family. He lives with his two brothers and two sisters, his mum and dad, his grandmother and grandfather and his uncle Bob. What a big family!
But Max is not happy. He is very small. His brothers and sisters laugh at him because he is so small. When they go to the shop for ice-cream Max can't go fast. "Ha, ha, ha!" they laugh, and they leave Max behind[1]. They are not nice to him and when they play basketball with their friends, he can often only watch.

[1] leave Max behind = Max zurücklassen

B. One day there is a bad storm. It rains and rains and rains. Water fills the river and soon it is very big and very fast and the water goes into the street.
Max's house is now an island[2]. There is water all around it.
It rains for six days. Everybody stays in the house and they eat all the food[3] in the house. After six days there is no food to eat.
"No food and no electricity[4]," says Max's father. "What can we do? Why can't I swim? Nobody[5] can swim in this family."

[2] island = Insel [5] nobody = keiner [4] electricity = Strom [3] food = Nahrung

C. Nobody? Max can swim. He has swimming lessons at school.
He looks at the fast river. Then he jumps into the water and starts to swim.
"Look!" shout his brothers and sisters. "Look at Max! He is swimming!"
Then Max is at the next house. This house has a telephone and he phones the police. After 30 minutes the police come in boats[6] and take the family to a dry place and give them food.
Max is very tired[7] but very happy. Everyone in the family is very proud[8] of him ... and they never leave him behind again.

[6] boats = Boote [7] tired = müde [8] proud = stolz

You can also listen to the CD. Track 5

1 Find the right endings.

Finde die richtigen Ergänzungen. Verbinde sie mit Linien.

Max	come and take the family to a dry place.
Max	rains for six days.
Max	has no electricity.
His brothers and sisters	can swim.
Then it	is no food in the house.
Soon there	is nine years old.
The house	is very small.
Only Max	lives with his family in a big house.
The police	can play basketball with his brothers and sister.
Now Max	often play basketball with friends.

2 Write the answers to these questions in your exercise book.

Schreibe die Antworten zu den folgenden Fragen in dein Heft.

Who ...

1. is Bob?
2. is the smallest in the family?
3 do Max's brothers and sisters play basketball with?
4. stays in the house?
5. can swim?
6. does Max phone?
7. is very happy?

Where ...

1. does Max live?
2 does Max jump?
3. does Max swim to?

3 Find all the information about Max from the text.
Now write about him in your exercise book. Start like this:
Finde die Informationen, die im Text über Max stehen. Schreibe in deinem Heft einen eigenen Text. So kannst du anfangen:

Max is ... years old. He has ... family. He is ...

4 Note taking – keywords – titles
Notizen machen – Schlüsselwörter – Überschriften

1. Read part **A** of the story again. Look at the underlined words. They are the important words in part **A**. You can use them to take notes.
   Lies Teil **A** noch einmal. Sieh dir die unterstrichenen Wörter an. Das sind Schlüsselwörter in Teil **A**. Du kannst sie benutzen, um dir Notizen zu machen.

2. Now underline the keywords in parts **B** and **C**.
   Unterstreiche nun die Schlüsselwörter in Teil **B** und **C**.

3. Find headings for **A**, **B**, and **C**.
   Finde Überschriften für Teil **A**, **B** und **C**. Hier findest du einige Ideen:

   Too small   Big family   What brothers and sisters!
   A bad storm!   ...

5 Say it in English.
Schreibe in dein Heft. Sage auf Englisch, dass ...

1. Max nicht glücklich ist.
2. er sehr stolz ist.
3. er sehr klein ist.
4. er nicht schnell ist.
5. er sehr müde ist.

2.2 Hören und verstehen

GOOD TO KNOW **Richtig ergänzen**

Gehe so vor:

- Bevor du ein Text anhörst, lies die Überschrift. Überlege, wovon der Text handeln könnte. Manchmal gibt es Bilder. Schau dir die Bilder an. Die Überschrift und die Bilder helfen dir beim Verstehen.
- Du kannst die CD mehrmals laufen lassen. Hör dir den Text an. Worum geht es?
- Lies die Aufgabe. Hör dir den Text noch einmal an.
- Erledige nun die Aufgabe.
- Hör dir den Text noch einmal an. Überprüfe deine Antworten.

In the street

Track 6

1 Listen to the noises and number the words from 1-10 when you hear them.

Höre dir die Geräusche an und nummeriere sie beim Zuhören von 1-10.

a lorry[1] a bird a car a German an old bike

a dog a train[2] a cat a motorbike a tram[3]

[1] lorry = Lastwagen
[2] train = Zug
[3] tram = Straßenbahn

2 Say it in English.

Schreibe in dein Heft. Sage auf Englisch, dass ...

Nummer eins ein (...) ist. Number one is a
Nummer vier ein (...) ist.
Nummer fünf kein (...) ist. Number five isn't a
Nummer acht kein (...) ist.

Traffic

Track 7

1 Listen to the CD and colour the picture.
Höre dir die CD an und male das Bild aus.

The street where I live

Track 8

1 Listen to the CD and tick (✓) the words that you hear.
Höre die CD an und setze einen Haken (✓) hinter die Wörter, die du hörst.

1. meet		street		6. big		pig	
2. fourteen		forty		7. floor		door	
3. bed		red		8. school		pool	
4. mouse		house		9. tree		three	
5. who		you		10. buy		fly	

2 Colour the doors in the correct colours.
Male die Türen in den richtigen Farben aus.

3 Right or wrong? Listen to the CD. Tick (✓) the box.
Richtig oder falsch? Setze einen Haken (✓) in das richtige Kästchen.

	wrong	right
1. Betty lives at number 16.		
2. Mr Brown lives at number 18.		
3. David lives at number 4.		
4. David's house has got a red door.		
5. Betty is a dog.		
6. Tommy's door is black.		

7. School finishes at four o'clock.
8. The children go into the supermarket after school.
9. They buy hamburgers in the supermarket.

4 Fill in the English words.

Trage die englischen Wörter in das Kreuzworträtsel ein.

Across →: 2 *aufhören, beenden* 6 *Tür* 7 *neben* (2 Wörter) 10 *Schokolade* 12 *wohnen, leben* 13 *kaufen* 14 *Nummer, Zahl, Ziffer*

Down ↓: 1 *Sandwich* 3 *Supermarkt* 4 *Schule* 5 *Strasse* 8 *Polizeihund* 9 *Polizist* 11 *Haus*

5 Say it in English.
Schreibe in dein Heft. Sage auf Englisch, ...

1. welche Farbe dein Haus hat.
2. welches deine Hausnummer ist.
3. dass dein Freund einen Hund hat.
4. dass dein Vater Polizist ist.
5. dass die Schule um 15 Uhr zu Ende ist.

My street

Track 9

1 Listen to the CD and finish the picture.
Höre die CD an und vervollständige das Bild.

2 **Look at your picture and listen to the CD again.**
Now find the answer to these questions. Write the answers in your exercise book.
Sieh dir dein Bild an und höre dir den Text noch einmal an. Beantworte nun die Fragen. Schreibe in dein Heft.

1. What animals can you see in the picture?
2. How many people are in the park?
3. What colour is the bus?
4. What colour is the Sunday bus to Hillend?
5. What is the name of the boy at the window?
6. Why is there only one tree in the park?
7. Who has got two dogs?

3 **These are places and buildings in town. Find the words.**
In diesen Zeilen sind Wörter versteckt. Die Dinge sind alle in einer Stadt zu finden. Schreibe die Wörter in dein Heft.

yypayyryyk *ydyyeyypyyartyyyymyenyt ysytoyre*

byyouyytiyyqyueyy *zyyyoyyyo* *yhyyoyyyuyysye*

syyupyyyeryymyayryket *byyoyoyk syyhoyyp* *gyayrayyyge*

reysytyayuyrayyynt *ciynyeyma* *syyyyychyyyyooyyl*

sywiymymyying pyyyoyol *reycyoyrd syhyoyp*

4 **Say it in English.**
Schreibe in dein Heft. Sage auf Englisch, dass ...

1. vor dem Haus ein Hund ist.
2. es nur einen Baum gibt.
3. es das einzige Fenster oben ist.
4. es auch einen grünen Bus gibt.
5. es einen Park gibt.

What is happening?

Track 10

1 Read the questions before you listen to the CD. Tick (✓) the right answer.

Lies zuerst die Fragen, höre dir dann den Text an und mache ein Häkchen(✓) hinter die richtige Antwort.

1. What day of the week is it?
   - It is Friday.
   - It is Saturday.
   - It is Sunday.

2. What are John and Sam doing? They are ...
   - washing the car.
   - playing football.
   - cutting the grass.

3. Where does Mrs Patterson's son live? He lives ...
   - in Austria.
   - in Australia.
   - in America.

4. Who likes the garden?
   - Mr Patterson likes the garden.
   - Mr Green likes the garden.
   - Tom likes the garden.

5. How old is Peggy? She is ...
   - fourteen.
   - four.
   - five.

6. Who gets a big letter?
   - Mrs Patterson gets a big letter.
   - The postman gets a big letter.
   - Mr Jackson gets a big letter.

2 **Find all the words from the text in the box.**

In diesem Suchrätsel sind 13 Wörter oder Wortgruppen in diesen Richtungen versteckt: → ↓ ↘. Finde und umkreise alle Wörter und schreibe sie in dein Heft.

R	E	E	N	Q	P	E	O	P	L	E	K	K	S	I
O	Q	F	O	E	P	G	C	L	P	X	G	U	J	H
A	X	Q	I	Q	A	L	C	M	C	S	O	S	X	V
D	A	O	S	B	X	L	A	R	A	N	O	N	M	J
K	H	B	Y	L	E	T	T	E	R	S	G	N	Z	B
K	J	M	E	M	S	G	Q	O	E	Y	R	N	K	C
D	R	A	W	I	N	G	P	I	C	T	U	R	E	S
U	L	P	O	S	T	M	A	N	T	P	V	A	F	B
C	U	T	T	I	N	G	T	H	E	G	R	A	S	S
P	L	A	Y	I	N	G	F	O	O	T	B	A	L	L
C	I	D	A	N	G	A	R	D	E	N	W	O	R	K

Die versteckten Wörter sind:

DRAWING PICTURES — CUTTING THE GRASS — GARDEN WORK
PLAYING FOOTBALL — LETTERS — POSTMAN — PEOPLE
NOISY — ROAD — SON — CAR

3 **Say it in English.**

Schreibe in dein Heft. Sage auf Englisch, dass ...

1. der Postbote sehr beschäftigt ist.
2. dein Freund in Amerika wohnt.
3. dein Vater den Rasen mäht.
4. es sehr laut ist.
5. er Gartenarbeit mag.

Father and daughter

Track 11

1 Answer this question before you listen to the CD.
Beantworte die folgende Frage, bevor du dir die CD anhörst.

Your mother or father has a free day. They don't work today. Where do you want to go together? The zoo? The park? The swimming pool? ...
I want to go to ______________ with my father or mother.

2 Listen to the text and tick (✓) the right answer.
Hör dir die CD an, und mache ein Häkchen (✓) an die richtige Antwort.

1. Where does the young girl want to go with her father?
   She wants to go ...
   - [ ] to the park.
   - [ ] to the cinema.
   - [ ] to the swimming pool.

2. Who are they going with? They are going with ...
   - [ ] the girl's mother.
   - [ ] the girl's best friend.
   - [ ] the girl's brother.

3. What time do you think they go to the cinema?
   - [ ] They go at 9:30 a.m.
   - [ ] They go at 12:45 p.m.
   - [ ] They go at 2 p.m.

4. What does the girl want to do after that?
   - [ ] She wants to swim in the park.
   - [ ] She wants to go to the beach.
   - [ ] She wants to go shopping.

5. What is the father's idea for the evening? They ...
   - [ ] go to a restaurant.
   - [ ] watch a film on TV.
   - [ ] play a computer game.

3 Listen to the CD again and mark the words that you hear.

Höre dir die CD noch einmal an, und mache ein Häkchen (✓) hinter die Wörter, die du hörst.

friends	cinema	tennis	TV
aunt	uncle	mother	father
stops	starts	time	hour
boring	interesting	meeting	hamburger
hot dog	popcorn	school	park
beach	restaurant	swimming pool	

4 Ask in English.

Frage auf Englisch, ...

1. ob du ins Kino gehen kannst.
2. welchen Film der Vater sehen möchte.
3. wann der Film anfängt.
4. ob du Popcorn haben darfst.
5. was ihr nach dem Film machen könnt.

Animals in my street

Track 12

1 Match the food and the animals. Do this before you listen to the CD.

Ordne den Tieren das Futter zu, das sie fressen. Verbinde die Wörter mit einem Strich. Löse diese Aufgabe, bevor du dir die CD anhörst.

mouse	*grass*
dog	*apples*
cat	*cheese*
horse	*meat*
pig	*fish*

2 Tick (✓) the right sentence.
Mache ein Häkchen (✓) an den richtigen Satz.

1. The cat's name is ...
   - Snowy.
   - Blacky.
   - Jenny.
2. The dog's name is ...
   - Linda.
   - Blacky.
   - Snowy.
3. - Blacky is black.
   - Blacky is brown.
   - Blacky is white.
4. - Jenny has got big, brown eyes.
   - Linda has got big, brown eyes.
   - The dog's eyes are brown.
5. - Snowy sometimes catches three balls.
   - Blacky sometimes catches three mice.
   - Snowy sometimes catches three mice.
6. - A cat and a mouse run out from behind the garden chairs.
   - Blacky and Snowy run out from behind the garden chairs.
   - A dog and a mouse run out from behind the garden chairs.
7. - Blacky is first, and Snowy is second.
   - The first mouse is black, and the second mouse is white.
   - Snowy is first, and Blacky is second.
8. Snowy is not happy because ...
   - Blacky has got her ball.
   - Blacky is in the bushes.
   - Blacky has got her mouse.

9. Blacky runs because ...
   - Snowy is not happy.
   - there is a mouse in front of Jenny.
   - he is hungry.

10.
   - Blacky gives the mouse to Snowy.
   - Snowy gives the mouse to Blacky.
   - Blacky eats the mouse.

3 Say it in English.
Schreibe in dein Heft. Sage auf Englisch, dass ...

1. Ann eine schwarze Katze mit grünen Augen hat.
2. Becky den Ball zu Jenny wirft.
3. die Katze nicht glücklich ist, weil der Hund ihre Maus hat.
4. die Katze die Maus frisst.
5. es ein Geschenk für deine Mutter ist.

An accident in my street

Track 13

1 Complete the text with the words from the box.
Vervollständige den Text mit den angebotenen Wörtern.

birthday *dangerous* *girl* *helmet (= Fahrradhelm)* *laugh* *silly*

Tim has got a new bike for his ____________. It is green and black. Ah, yes, and a new ____________, too. His mum says he must wear it all the time. The streets are ____________. Tim doesn't like it. He thinks it is ____________. His friends will ____________ at him and say, "Tim is a ____________."

2 **Now listen to the CD and check your answers.**
Höre dir jetzt die CD an und überprüfe deine Antworten.

3 **Listen to the CD again and answer the questions.**
Höre dir jetzt die CD noch einmal an und beantworte die Fragen. Schreibe die Antworten in dein Heft.

1. Where is Tim going?
2. How far is it?
3. Who is with him?
4. What is Tim wearing?
5. Is Bob wearing that, too?

4 **Find the two parts of the sentences. Write the sentences in your exercise book.**
Finde die Satzteile, die zusammengehören. Verbinde Zusammengehörendes mit Linien. Schreibe die vollständigen Sätze in dein Heft.

1. Tim got a new bike	the police.
2. Tim doesn't like	dangerous.
3. The streets are	next to the library.
4. Bob is not	for his birthday.
5. The boys fall	onto the ground.
6. Tim phones	his helmet.
7. The restaurant is	wearing a helmet.

5 **Say it in English.**
Schreibe in dein Heft. Sage auf Englisch, dass ...

1. es zehn Minuten mit dem Fahrrad zur Schule ist.
2. die Straßen gefährlich sind.
3. du im Moment einen Helm trägst.
4. das Restaurant neben der Bibliothek ist.

Where can I go?

Track 14

1 **Before you listen to the CD, draw a line from the words on the right to the places on the left.**
Bevor du den Text auf der CD anhörst, zeichne eine Linie von den Wörtern auf der rechten Seite zu den passenden Wörtern auf der linken Seite.

toy shop	*chips*
bike shop	*ticket*
book shop	*stamp*
cinema	*dominoes*
music shop	*bike bag*
pet shop	*MP3 player*
post office	*magazine*
restaurant	*dog food*

2 **Now listen to the CD and answer the questions. Write the answers in your exercise book.**
Nun höre dir den Text auf der CD an und beantworte die Fragen. Schreibe die Antworten in dein Heft.

1. What does Tom want to buy?
2. Where is he going on holiday?
3. How long is the car trip?
4. How much money has he got?
5. What is the name of the shop?
   - It is Sky Diver. ☐
   - It is Sky Hi. ☐
   - It is Sky Fly. ☐
   - It is MP3 Hi. ☐
6. When do the two friends want to go to the shop?
7. How do they want to go to the shop?

8. What time must Janet be home?
9. Why?

3 Listen to the CD again and tick (✓) the sentences from the CD.

Höre dir den Text noch einmal an und mache ein Häkchen (✓) hinter die Sätze, die im Text vorkommen.

1. You go shopping every Saturday with your dad.
   You go shopping every Saturday with your mum.
2. Can you tell me where to buy a new MP3 player?
   Can you tell me where to get a new MP3 player?
3. Dad says it is 18 hours by car.
   Dad says it is 16 hours by car.
4. My old MP3 player is good.
   My old MP3 player is not good.
5. But their things are cheap.
   But their things are not cheap.
6. It's my birthday money.
   It's my Christmas money.
7. I must be home at 5 o'clock.
   I must be home at 7 o'clock.

4 Ask in English.

Frage auf Englisch, ...

1. wie es jemandem geht.
2. wo du eine neue Federmappe kaufen kannst.
3. ob jemand genug Geld hat.
4. wann jemand kommen kann.
5. warum jemand einen neuen MP3-Spieler braucht.
6. wie das Geschäft heißt.
7. warum jemand um fünf Uhr zu Hause sein muss.

People in my street

Track 15

1 **Before you listen to the CD, write the words under the pictures.**
Bevor du dir die CD anhörst, schreibe die passenden Wörter unter die Bilder.

bus driver
nurse
teacher
policeman
postman
window cleaner

2 **Now listen to the CD and fill in the information.**
Höre dir jetzt die CD an und trage die Informationen in die Tabelle ein.

Name	age	job	pets	family	like / not like
Mary Martin					
Peter Price					
Mrs Kerr					
Mr Townsend					

3 **Who thinks what? Write the names after the sentences.**
Wer denkt was? Schreibe den Namen hinter den Satz.

EXAMPLE

Pamela must take the dog out now. *Mrs Martin*

1. I want a dog, too.
2. Look! There are those loud children again!
3. Now where are my cats? Ah, yes, up the tree again.
4. I like to play football in the afternoon with my son.
5. I hope that there isn't a lot of traffic on the road today.
6. It is raining but I must go out with Jack.
7. I can't sleep because the children are so loud.
8. It is great that I don't go to work any more. I can sleep until 10 o'clock in the morning.

4 **Say it in English.**
Schreibe in dein Heft. Sage auf Englisch, dass ...

1. du einen Hund haben möchtest.
2. es ein Scherz ist.
3. du schlafen möchtest.
4. Rover ein wirklich netter Hund ist.
5. du Sport liebst.
6. der Garten zu klein ist.
7. du keine Zeit für Tiere hast.

5 **Fill in this table about you and a friend.**
Ergänze die Tabelle mit Informationen über dich selbst und einen Freund / eine Freundin.

Name	age	hobby	pets	family	like / not like

6 Fill in the crossword. All the words are from the CD.

Trage die richtigen Wörter in das Kreuzworträtsel ein. Alle Wörter kommen im Text auf der CD vor.

Across →:

5 nachts *6 Freunde* *7 keine Zeit* *10 Polizist*
12 Mountainbike *13 Lehrer/Lehrerin*
14 Busfahrer/Busfahrerin

Down↓:

1 Kaninchen *2 Fensterputzer* *3 Kinder* *4 Sohn*
8 Haustier *9 Apfelbaum* *11 laut*

3 Schreiben

Das musst du am Ende der Klasse 5 können:

- Eine einfache Postkarte oder E-Mail schreiben, z. B. mit Feriengrüßen
- Einen Steckbrief über dich oder andere schreiben
- Einfache Sätze schreiben
- Eine Mindmap zu einem bestimmten Thema erstellen
- Kurze Gedichte schreiben
- Einen Text nach einer Vorlage schreiben
- Deinen Stundenplan auf Englisch schreiben

3.1 Wortfeldarbeit

GOOD TO KNOW **Mindmaps nutzen**

Bevor du einen Text schreibst, sammle Stichwörter für deinen Text. Hierfür kannst du eine **Mindmap** erstellen. Schreibe zunächst Oberbegriffe auf und danach Unterbegriffe.
Mindmap bedeutet Gedankenkarte. In der Mitte steht der Hauptbegriff, davon zweigen wie auf einer Karte die Oberbegriffe ab. Diese verzweigen sich weiter. Dort stehen die Unterbegriffe.

Tipps für das Schreiben:

- Schreibe zuerst kurze, einfache Sätze auf.
- Du kannst einen Text, einen Brief oder eine Postkarte aus dem Buch als Muster nehmen.
- Überlege dir eine Überschrift.
- Fange nicht jeden Satz gleich an.
- Verbinde Sätze mit and oder but.

1 Put these words into a mindmap.

Schreibe die Wörter in eine Mindmap zum Thema school hinein.

school

canteen classroom English German

maths pupils subjects teachers timetable

uniform rooms people gym break

2 **What belongs where? Write the correct numbers in the boxes. There are some words that do not belong. Put a cross in the boxes.**
Was gehört wozu? Es gibt einige Wörter, die nicht dazugehören. Setze ein Kreuz in die Kästchen dieser Wörter.

1. *my pencil case* 2. *school bag* 3. *my books* 4. *my snacks*

☐ *an apple* ☐ *a biro* ☐ *a bottle of water* ☐ *a cake*
☐ *an exercise book* ☐ *a felt-tip* ☐ *a folder* ☐ *a pen*
☐ *a pencil* ☐ *a pencil sharpener* ☐ *a phone* ☐ *a ruler*
☐ *a rubber* ☐ *a sandwich* ☐ *a shirt* ☐ *a tennis ball*
☐ *a textbook* ☐ *a yoyo*

3 **Make a mindmap with your own words for your classroom.**
Erstelle eine Mindmap mit Dingen aus deinem Klassenzimmer.

A language school

1 **Underline all the words for things that you can find in your classroom.**
Unterstreiche alle Bezeichnungen für Gegenstände, die in deinem Klassenzimmer vorhanden sind.

board *book* *CD player* *chair* *clock* *computer*
cupboard *desk* *door* *exercise book* *floor*
noticeboard *pencil case* *poster* *rubber* *ruler*
school bag *timetable* *TV* *wall* *window*

2 **Look at the picture and fill in the table.**

Schau dir das Bild an und fülle die Tabelle aus.

Name		how old
Michael		
Marcus		
Susanna		
Andrew		
Waync		

3 **Write four sentences each about Tim, Robert, Hannah and yourself. Read the example first.**
Schreibe je vier Sätze über Tim, Robert, Hannah und dich. Lies zuerst das Beispiel.

EXAMPLE

Mia – ten – nice – not London / Liverpool – English
Mia is ten. She is nice. She isn't from London. She is from Liverpool. She is English.

1. Tim – eleven – funny – not Leeds/Manchester – Manchester United fan.
2. Robert – eleven – German – not Frankfurt/Berlin – Quentin Blake School.
3. Hannah – nine – good at sports – not English/German – in year 6.
4. You – how old? – are you English? Are you German? football fan? school?

4 **Answer Wayne's questions.**
Beantworte Waynes Fragen. Trage die Antworten ein.

Hello, what is your name?

My name is ______ .

Where are you from?

I am from ______ .

How old are you?

I am ______ .

How old is your best friend?

She is ______ .

Where is she from?

She is/comes from ____________________ .

What is her name?

Her name is ____________________ .

5 **Read what Wayne says. Then write a text about one of the other children in exercise 2.**

Lies, was Wayne sagt. Dann schreibe einen Text über eines der anderen Kinder in dein Heft.

Hello. My name is Wayne. I'm 12 years old. I'm from America. My friend's name is Marcus. He's from Germany. He's 11 years old.

6 **Read what Peggy, another pupil, says. Then write about yourself. Use (or change) the underlined words.**

Lies, was Peggy, eine andere Schülerin, sagt. Schreibe dann über dich, indem du alle unterstrichenen Wörter beibehältst oder ersetzt.

My name is Peggy. I am eleven years old. I live in London. I have got one brother but I haven't got a sister. My brother's name is Tom and he is six years old. We have got a cat. Our cat is twelve years old. I like my school. English is my favourite subject. But I hate maths.

7 **Read Cassidy's email to you from Canada. Underline her questions and answer her mail.**

Lies Cassidys E-Mail aus Kanada. Unterstreiche ihre Fragen und beantworte ihre E-Mail. Schreibe in dein Heft.

My name is Cassidy Gale. What is your name? I am eleven years old. I live in Edmonton. That is in Canada. How old are you? Where are you from? Where is that? I'm in year 7 and my class teacher is Mr Black. My favourite subject is English and I hate maths. What is your favourite subject? Do you hate maths, too? Our school starts at 9 o'clock and it finishes at 3 o'clock. We often have sports in the afternoon. I love sports. In winter I play

icehockey and in summer I go swimming. The boys play American football in summer. I have lunch at school. All my friends have lunch at school. Sometimes it is not very good but usually it is OK. What about you? When does your school start and finish? Do you have lunch at school? What sports do you do? Oh, yes, and how do you get to school? I get to school by bus. We have big yellow school buses here.
Please write soon and answer my questions.
Goodbye. Cassidy

8 Say it in English.
Schreibe in dein Heft. Sage auf Englisch, ...

1. wie du heißt.
2. wie alt du bist.
3. wo du wohnst.
4. was dein Lieblingsfach ist.
5. welches Fach du hasst.

9 Look at the language school timetable for the English class.
Sieh dir den Stundenplan und das Beispiel an. Schreibe dann über zwei andere Tage.

Monday	Tuesday	Wednesday	Thursday	Friday
reading	reading	writing	reading	writing
writing	games	reading	grammar	reading
singing	singing	reading	grammar	singing
L	U	N	C	H
golf	hockey	golf	swimming	hockey
tennis	golf	tennis	swimming	hockey

EXAMPLE

On Monday the pupils have reading, writing and singing in the morning. After lunch they play golf and tennis.

My classroom

1 Read the sentences and write on the desks who sits where.
Lies die Sätze und schreibe auf die Tische, wer wo sitzt.

Bob is sitting next to the door.
Peter is sitting between John and Mandy in the first row.
John is not sitting next to Bob.
Jane is sitting behind Mandy.
Mary is sitting behind Peter and next to Linda.
Jack is sitting behind Jane, in the third row.
Jack is sitting between two girls.
Martin is sitting behind Carol. He is in the fourth row.
In the last row, the fifth row, Brian is sitting behind Martin. Pamela is sitting next to him, behind Max.
Steve is sitting next to Max and Janet is sitting in front of him.

2 **Make a drawing of the desks in your classroom. Then write a text like the one above (p. 97).**
Zeichne die Sitzordnung in deinem Klassenzimmer. Schreibe dann einen Text wie oben (S. 97).

Things in the classroom

1 **Write two dialogues using things on the pictures.**
Schreibe zwei Dialoge, in denen die abgebildeten Dinge vorkommen.

EXAMPLE

What's in my hand?
Is it a book? No, it isn't.
Is it a ruler? No, it isn't.
Is it an exercise book? No, it isn't.
It is a pencil case!

1.

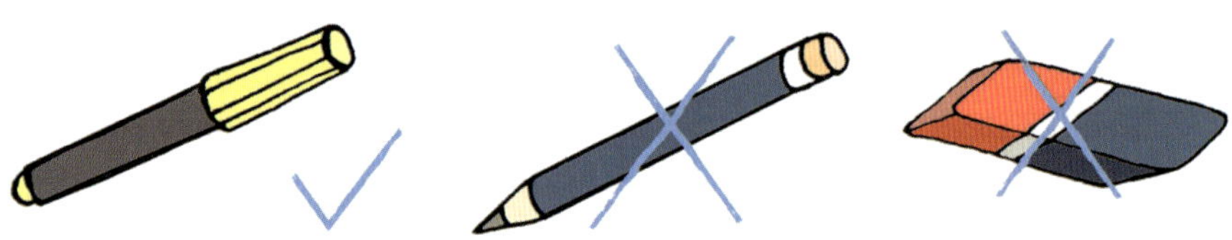

2.

REMEMBER *There is – there are*

Du schreibst there is a ... beim Singular (Einzahl).
Du schreibst there are ... beim Plural (Mehrzahl).
Sowohl there is als auch there are wird im Deutschen übersetzt mit „es gibt“.

2 Look at the classroom and write eight sentences. Use *there is* and *there are.*

Schau dir das Klassenzimmer an, und schreibe acht Sätze darüber. Benutze dafür *there is* und *there are.*

EXAMPLE

In this classroom there is a computer.

3 Say it in English.

Schreibe in dein Heft. Sage auf Englisch, dass ...

1. es in deiner Schule einen großen Schulhof gibt.
2. es einen Bus von deinem Haus bis zur Schule gibt.
3. es in deiner Schule 1100 Schüler gibt.
4. es in deiner Schule jede Woche eine Schulversammlung gibt.
5. es in deiner Schule 101 Lehrer gibt.

4 Write your name, one line for each letter. Then try and find a word connected with school for each letter.

Schreibe deinen Namen von oben nach unten. Versuche nun, ein Wort aus der Schule für jeden Buchstaben zu finden.

EXAMPLE

SANDRA:

S*chool bag*
A*rt*
N*otice board*
D*oor*
R*uler*
A*ssembly*

5 Read the text. Then write your own text. You can be a book or a school bag.

Lies den Text. Dann schreibe deinen eigenen Text. Entweder bist du ein Buch oder eine Schultasche.

I am a pencil case. There are lots of pencils in me. There is a blue pencil and a red pencil. There are two black pencils and a yellow pencil. There is a new red pencil sharpener and an old rubber. My rubber is black and yellow. My ruler is not big. I live in a school bag. I go to school from Monday to Friday. My owner is very nice. Her name is Pauline and she is 10 years old.

6 Find a partner to play this game.

Finde einen Partner. Spielt dieses Schulspiel.

Regeln: Entscheidet euch, ob ihr Schulsachen sammeln möchtet oder Gegenstände im Klassenraum. Würfelt abwechselnd. Landest du auf einem Feld mit einem Bild von etwas, das du sammelst, schreib den Begriff auf. Danach musst du einen Satz damit bilden. Du bekommst einen Punkt für jedes Wort in deinem Satz. Je länger dein Satz ist, desto mehr Punkte bekommst du. Dann ist dein Partner an der Reihe. Gewonnen hat derjenige, der als erster 100 Punkte erreicht hat.

EXAMPLE

I have got a new pencil in my pencil case. (10 Punkte).

7 Throw a dice and form a sentence.

Würfele dir einen Satz zusammen. Spiele mit einem Partner. Für die Zahl, die du würfelst, darfst du ein Wort aus der jeweiligen Spalte nehmen. Wo ein ? steht, darfst du ein Wort deiner Wahl ergänzen. Wer würfelt sich die meisten Sätze in zehn Minuten zusammen?

Regeln: Du würfelst erst eine 3, dann schreibst du have. Um den Satz zu vervollständigen, muss du eine 1, eine 5 und eine 6 würfeln. Jeder Satz muss mit In my classroom anfangen.

1	2	3	4	5	6
I you we they	he she	have	has	a two ?	?

8 Make sentences.

Bilde 6 Sätze aus Wörtern aus diesem Kasten.

→ The	boys	and	play	park	after
lose.	in	football	it	the	school.
they	my	like	every	in	But ↓
when	class	Their ↓	day	very	the
happy	the	team	good.	are	girls
not	girls,	against	always	they	don't
are	the	hockey	wins.	and	play
boys	girls	play	When ↓	hockey	football.
The ↑	win.	boys	the	play	← They

Timetables

1 Read the text and fill in the timetable.
Lies den Text und fülle den Stundenplan aus.

Linda: This is my timetable. Wednesday is my best day. The first and second lessons I have art[1]. Then I have English. Then there is the break. After the break I have two lessons of sports, then one lesson of maths.

Friday is a terrible day. The first lesson is maths, the second and the third lessons are geography. After break, the fourth lesson is music. Music is not my favourite lesson. The fifth lesson is R.E.[2] and the sixth lesson is French. On Monday I have English in the first lesson and in the fifth lesson. The second lesson is geography. The third lesson is maths and the fourth lesson is maths, too. The sixth lesson is sports.

On Tuesday I have French in the first and second lessons. The third and fourth lessons are English. The fifth lesson is maths and the sixth lesson is music. On Thursday I have art in the first lesson, history[3] in the second and third lessons and geography in the fourth lesson. In the fifth lesson I have English and in the sixth lesson I have R.E.

[1] art – Kunst
[2] R.E. = Religion
[3] history = Geschichte

Monday	Tuesday	Wednesday	Thursday	Friday
1				
2				
3				
B	R	E	A	K
4				
5				
6				

You can also listen to the CD. Track 16

2 Say it in English.
Schreibe in dein Heft. Sage auf Englisch, dass ...

1. du dienstags zwei Stunden Sport hast.
2. du nach der Pause am Mittwoch Mathe hast.
3. die erste Stunde am Montag Kunst ist.
4. Kunst nicht dein Lieblingsfach ist.
5. du in der fünften Stunde am Donnerstag Erdkunde hast.

3 Write about your best day and your worst day.
Schreibe jetzt über deinen besten Tag der Woche und deinen schlimmsten Tag.

EXAMPLE

My best day is ... because
.... is a terrible day because ...

4 Fill in the table with as many things as possible.
Schreibe möglichst viele Dinge in die Tabelle.

good things about school	not so good things about school

5 **Now use your ideas to write a short article for a students' magazine.**
Schreibe jetzt mithilfe deiner Ideen einen kurzen Artikel für eine Schülerzeitschrift. So kannst du anfangen:

EXAMPLE

What I like about school is ...
What I don't like about school is ...

6 **A crossword**

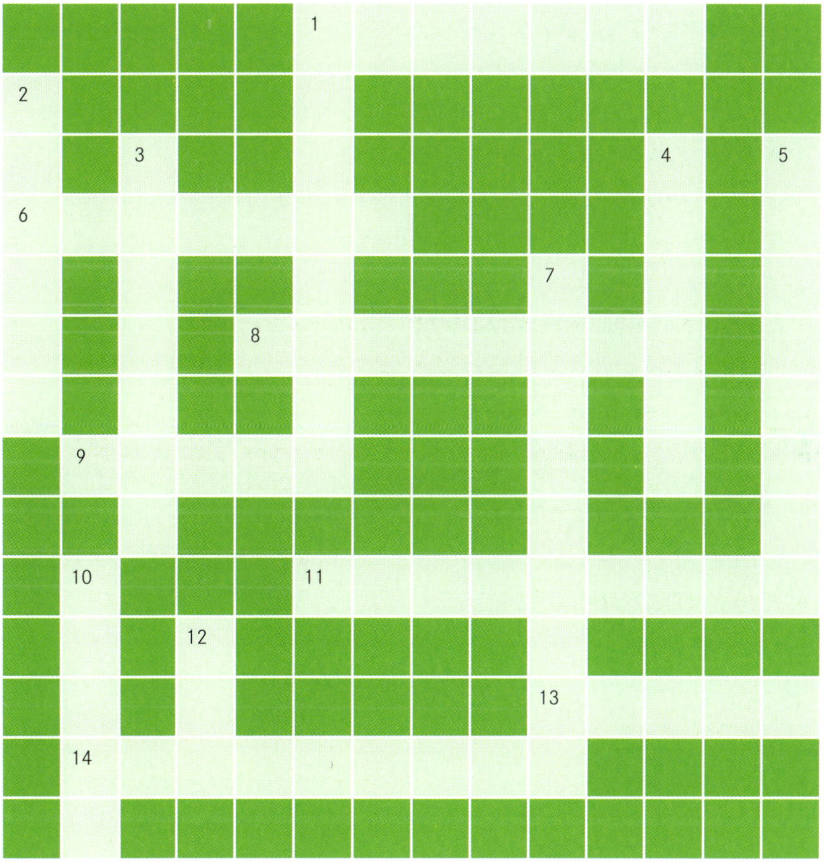

Across → :

1. In this subject you learn about the past. (= die Vergangenheit)
6. This is where you can eat lunch.
8. This is the best time. In the summer it is 6 weeks long.
9. This is the time at school when you have no lesson. It is usually about 20 minutes long.
11. In this subject you learn about different countries.
13. The number before fourth.
14. This tells you what subject you have and when.

Down ↓ :

1. This is work for school you do at home.
2. The number before 13 across.
3. The name for the clothes that children in Britain wear at school.
4. The English word for "Unterrichtsstunde".
5. The name for when all the children at school meet in a hall.
7. The subject I like best is my ... subject.
10. The number after fourth.
12. The big hall where you do sports.

7 Write about these four friends.

Schreibe über diese vier Freunde.

1. Das Bild zeigt, in welcher Klasse sie sind, welches ihre Lieblingsfächer sind, welche Fächer sie nicht mögen und welchen Sport sie mögen. Fülle zuerst die Tabelle aus.

name	year	favourite sport	favourite subject	not favourite subject

2. Schreibe jetzt einen Text über die Kinder in dein Heft.

EXAMPLE

Colin is in year seven. He plays tennis. He likes Maths. It is his favourite subject. He doesn't like English. It is not his favourite subject.

3.2 Erzählen zu einer Bildgeschichte

1 Connect the pictures and the sentences.

1. Ordne den Sätzen die passenden Bilder zu. Trage die richtige Nummer ein.

- She does her homework in the dining room.
- She goes to bed at half past eight.
- She goes to school by bus.
- She has breakfast in the kitchen.
- In the evening she watches TV.
- After the break it is geography.
- Maths is the first lesson.
- Lara gets up at 7 o'clock.
- She gets to school at a quarter to nine.
- Lara hates maths.
- She gets home at 4 o'clock.
- Lara likes geography.
- She goes home at half past three.
- She plays with her friends at break.

2. Schreibe die Sätze in der richtigen Reihenfolge in dein Heft.

2 Write your own story in your exercise book.
Schreibe deine eigene Geschichte in dein Heft.

Test

1 Read the postcard which Marcus wrote to his parents from his school trip.

Lies die Postkarte, die Marcus von seiner Klassenfahrt an seine Eltern geschrieben hat.

Dear Mum and Dad,
I am having a great time here at Silverton Castle. I am in a room with seven boys. The boys can sleep in the castle. Our window is the window with the X on the picture. The girls must sleep in another house. The food is OK but the breakfast is early – 8 o'clock! Today we are going to make a rally in Silverton. Then we can go shopping. There is a good ice-cream shop in the town. The weather is warm but windy.
See you on Friday.
Love, Marcus

1. Mache ein Häkchen (✔) an die Dinge, über die Marcus schreibt.

weather	☐	rooms	☐	sports	☐
food	☐	beds	☐	activities	☐
jobs	☐	games	☐	disco	☐
time for bed	☐	boys and girls	☐	jokes	☐

2. Schreibe jetzt eine andere Postkarte. Verwende folgende Informationen:

nice weather *food* *number of rooms* *friends* *sports*
boys and girls *teachers* *shopping* *pocket money* *disco*